MAKING WORK WORK

MAKING WORK WORK

The Positivity Solution for Any Work Environment

SHOLA RICHARDS

STERLING ETHOS
New York

STERLING ETHOS
New York

An Imprint of Sterling Publishing Co., Inc.
1166 Avenue of the Americas
New York, NY 10036

ISBN 978-1-4549-1872-1

Library of Congress Cataloging-in-Publication Data

Names: Richards, Shola, author.
Title: Making work work : the positivity solution for any work environment / Shola Richards.
Description: New York City : Sterling Ethos, 2016. | Includes bibliographical references and index.
Identifiers: LCCN 2016016626 | ISBN 9781454918721 (hardback)
Subjects: LCSH: Work environment. | Self-actualization (Psychology) | BISAC: SELF-HELP / Personal Growth / Success. | BUSINESS & ECONOMICS / Workplace Culture. | BUSINESS & ECONOMICS / Management.
Classification: LCC HD7261 .R4967 2016 | DDC 658.3/12--dc23
LC record available at https://lccn.loc.gov/2016016626

Distributed in Canada by Sterling Publishing Co., Inc.
c/o Canadian Manda Group, 664 Annette Street
Toronto, Ontario, Canada M6S 2C8
Distributed in the United Kingdom by GMC Distribution Services
Castle Place, 166 High Street, Lewes, East Sussex, England BN7 1XU
Distributed in Australia by NewSouth Books
45 Beach Street, Coogee, NSW 2034, Australia

For information about custom editions, special sales, and premium and corporate purchases, please contact Sterling Special Sales at 800-805-5489 or specialsales@sterlingpublishing.com.

Manufactured in the United States of America

2 4 6 8 10 9 7 5 3 1

www.sterlingpublishing.com

For my parents,

Laura and Josephus Richards

In every way, you showed me that it was always possible to make my life work, even during the most challenging times. I owe everything to you both. This one is for you.

Contents

Introduction

I almost killed myself.

Just to be clear, I'm not talking about accidentally doing this—I'm talking about a very real time in my life when I gave some serious consideration to *intentionally and purposefully* taking my own life.

I've never shared this with anyone before. People who know me personally are probably finding this information incredibly shocking. After all, I'm the guy with the perpetual smile on his face, the champion of all things positive, and a person with a love of life that most people would be hard-pressed to match.

While that's all true today, there was a time in my life when I honestly believed that the *only* solution to healing the deep, festering, and very well-hidden wounds of my soul was suicide. I can promise you that positivity wouldn't have even made the Top 100 of viable solutions for the broken heap that was my life at the time.

What went wrong? It's not that I was mentally ill, grew up neglected and abused, or ever struggled with depression. Suicidal thoughts aren't supposed to come to people like me, right?

That's what I thought, too, but I was very wrong. I learned a lot about myself on the day those thoughts paid me an unexpected visit, and it's from the pain and utter desperation of that suicidal moment that the book you're about to read was born.

Like millions of people in this world, my story begins with an experience that far too many of us can relate to: going to work at a soul-destroying job.

THE NEAR DEADLY DECISION

I'm no stranger to terrible jobs. If you can think of a workplace horror story, I'd be willing to wager an ice-cold beer of your choice that I've experienced something that is equally as bad, or I have witnessed someone else on the wrong end of something that is equally as bad.

Vicious bullying, physical violence, sexual harassment, overt racism and sexism, egregious abuses of power, constant rudeness and incivility—you name it and I've seen it in my career. Unfortunately, that's exactly the problem. For me, it was impossible to witness this type of behavior on a consistent basis without losing a sizable chunk of faith in the human race each time it happened.

Over ten years ago, I worked at a particularly horrific job, one that gave me a front-row seat for most of the life-destroying behaviors mentioned above. I also witnessed the effects that those behaviors can have on people, including me.

Most of my coworkers at this particular job seemed resigned to the pitiful fate of spending each day dodging the bullies, accepting deep-seated job dissatisfaction, and judging their day's success on whether they remained sane by the five o'clock quitting time. Each day started with the same sorry goal in mind: survival. On and on it went: Lather, rinse, repeat. It didn't take me long to realize that jobs like this only had one purpose—to slowly strip the humanity away from each of us until we unwillingly became helpless and mindless zombies.

I believed that this pitiful fate was not going to happen to me. *I will* never *become a zombie like them*, I would say to myself defiantly as I looked down my nose at the broken souls in the cubicles next to me. Unfortunately for me, even though I fought valiantly, as the weeks turned into months and the months turned into years, I could feel my humanity slowly slipping away with each passing day that I worked there.

It is very challenging for me to explain how I felt each morning when the alarm clock went off in preparation for another workday. But the best way to describe that sickening feeling is *soul-destroying pain.*

That is not meant for dramatic effect.

Each day before work, I would sit in the parking lot and stare at my watch (which was perfectly synchronized with the office clock), and literally wait for the last possible second before I would leave my car and pitifully drag myself inside the office to deal with three spirit-crushing constants for eight hours straight: (1) being treated in a subhuman fashion by the leadership, (2) being expected to happily accept any and all forms of horrific customer abuse or risk being fired, and (3) dealing with a toxic culture of bullying, incivility, gossip, and backstabbing from 90 percent of the people who worked there.

With the exception of my first month on the job, I dealt with the aforementioned reality of that miserable existence every day I worked there. And I worked there for *two long years*. I might still even be there if it weren't for the life-changing, and nearly life-ending, moment that completely transformed me forever.

When my alarm clock went off on that nondescript autumn morning, I noticed something that was very different about me. Instead of feeling the usual fear, dread, or soul-destroying pain that were my constant companions for close to two years, all those feelings had mysteriously vanished.

Little did I know it at the time, but this was not a good thing.

Instead of feeling pain, I woke up feeling nothing. My pain was replaced by complete and utter emptiness. It was such a bizarre feeling, and unless you've ever felt complete emotional emptiness before, you might not grasp what you're about to read. Absolutely nothing mattered to me anymore. My job didn't matter to me. My girlfriend (who is now my lovely wife and the mother of my two equally lovely little girls) didn't matter to me. My parents, friends, and loved ones didn't matter to me. My happiness didn't matter to me. My life didn't matter to me.

On that day, I knew what it was like to have my soul destroyed.

The normally enthusiastic, life-of-the-party, and boundlessly energetic guy who loved to make everyone smile was effectively dead inside. I officially became one of the company's soulless zombies who would mindlessly support its mission until I was too old and broken down to do it anymore. The company had won and I had lost. Even though I was fully aware of this fact, and even though I swore that I would never become one of the company's zombies, at that point, I was too emotionally devastated to care.

And that was far from the worst of my problems.

As I drove in to work that autumn morning, for the first and only time in my life, extremely terrifying thoughts crept into my mind as I drove down the I-405 freeway in Los Angeles:

You should just drive your car off the freeway overpass. Come on man, just turn the wheel and gun the accelerator. Seriously, just do it and get it over with. Your life doesn't matter to anyone. You need to make the pain stop. DO IT.

These weren't just passing thoughts, mind you. These were strong impulses. I almost heeded the deadly siren's call, too. Why shouldn't I? I had just turned thirty, which meant that I had at least another thirty years of dealing with this incredibly bleak future ahead of me. There was no escape for me. I couldn't become an actor, a professional basketball player, or a singer—I didn't have the talent to do any of those things. Even if I quit, I would just end up replacing this soul-sucking job with another soul-sucking job. It would be no different from rearranging the deck chairs on the sinking *Titanic* as far as I was concerned.

That's when it became clear. The only options available to me were to either win the lottery, learn to accept a life of workplace misery for the next thirty-plus years, or kill myself. That was it. And in that moment, only one of those options made sense.

So, I sharply turned the steering wheel toward the guardrail.

THE REBIRTH AND THE NEW SOLUTION

Thankfully, as I turned the wheel toward the guardrail, something made me regain control of my senses and wildly swerve back onto the freeway. To this day, I don't know what enabled me to fight through those dark thoughts and continue to drive to work that morning. But when I finally made it to the parking lot, I absolutely lost it as I slumped over the steering wheel of my car and started to cry as no adult has ever cried before.

Trust me, I'm talking about the ugly cry—complete with an endless flow of snot running out my nose, both eyes puffy and bloodshot, and coughing to the point at which I was barely able to breathe. Unlike before, this was a good thing. That was all the proof I needed that I wasn't completely emotionally dead.

Not yet, anyway.

At that point, I knew exactly what I had to do. I cleaned up my face, slammed my car door, and walked into the office with a single-minded purpose to do what I should have done eighteen months earlier. I powered up my computer, typed up my resignation letter, submitted it to my boss, and two weeks later I walked away from my job without another job lined up and without a sizable savings account to fall back on.

Thankfully, I didn't leave that company empty-handed. When I walked away from that job for the very last time, I had two things in my possession that were far more valuable than another job or thousands of dollars in savings.

I left with my sanity and my new mission.

As my humanity returned to me in the coming months, I felt a very real need to do something with my new lease on life. I couldn't be the only person who felt hopelessly trapped in a toxic job and who endured enormous emotional pain because of it. After doing a little research, I realized that there weren't just a few people who felt this intense pain on a daily basis as I did—there were literally millions of people who were fighting for their humanity each day at work.

My mission was clear: I needed to fix the problems in the workplace. As quickly as I came up with my new mission, I came up with the solution:

We need to treat each other better. Period.

WHY I'M WRITING THIS BOOK

I believe there is a natural tendency to overcomplicate how to solve big problems. And, make no mistake, healing the problems facing the modern workplace is *Tyrannosaurus Rex* big. While that's true, the problems are still solvable and can be done in a very simple manner. The latest workplace fads, cool-kid business trends, and other silliness won't be needed here.

The solution lies in finding people—or, better yet, becoming the person—with the courage to lead with a spirit of positivity. This is how we will finally make our workplaces work.

What does this mean, exactly? It means building a solid foundation in our workplaces based on kindness and mutual respect. It means directly addressing the incivility and bullying in our workplaces, instead of waiting for an imaginary hero to fly in and save us from them. It means building a workplace culture that promotes accountability, appreciation, support, and trust. It means leading by example and leaving a legacy of meaningful work for the people who come after us. These strategies, among many others, will be presented in the following pages, along with actionable plans to make them reality.

Are you up for the challenge?

Good. Because I need you. The world needs you. We are going to create a workplace movement starting today, and if you think that you need a title of supervisor, manager, or director to participate, you are mistaken. All you need is an open mind, a healthy dose of resilience, and some guts. I'll provide everything else.

I believe that creating a more positive work experience is possible for you, me, and anyone else who picks up this book and follows the strategies outlined in these pages. In a sense, I'm almost daring you to prove me wrong. If you deeply desire a more positive workplace than the one you're currently dragging yourself to for forty-plus hours a week, you have absolutely nothing to lose by putting these tools into action and being part of this movement. We both know that doing nothing, buying lottery tickets each week in hopes that you'll find a way out of your current situation, chronically complaining about your job, or driving into a guardrail aren't the real solutions to your problems.

The solution is to sincerely and consistently treat ourselves and others with kindness, respect, and positivity. These are not activities that are separate from doing the real work. *This* is *the real work.* It is actually the only work that matters and ever will matter.

I'll spend the following pages proving it to you.

SECTION

1

THE REAL WORK

Why Positivity is the Solution

CHAPTER

1

SUNSHINE, RAINBOWS, AND KITTENS

Exploding the Myths of Positivity

In order to carry a positive action,
we must develop here a positive vision.

—DALAI LAMA

Borrowing from the late Dr. Martin Luther King, Jr., I have a dream, too.

My dream is to create a more deeply meaningful, productive, and positive workplace experience for all of us. Yes, you read that right—*all of us.* I feel safe in assuming that most people think I'm setting my sights way too high or I'm fighting for a dream that most people believe is completely impossible.

I am asking you not to be like most people.

Contrary to popular belief, it is not impossible to positively transform the working world in a large-scale way. Difficult? Absolutely. Impossible? No. That is the goal that we will be dealing with head-on in this book.

Fair warning, though: If you think this goal is impossible, you are probably not ready for what you are about to read. That's perfectly okay. Before we get too deeply into this, my advice at this point would be to put the book down and walk away—I promise I won't be offended. The only prerequisite to continuing on is a mind that is slightly open to the idea that it is possible to succeed when so many others have failed.

Still here? Good.

Since you're still with me, I'm going to lay out a case for the critical need for positivity in our workplaces, starting today. If you've picked up this book, hopefully that means that you recognize this desperate need, too. Maybe you have been emotionally battered by a toxic work environment, and you are desperate to reclaim your career, your happiness, and, most of all, your life. Maybe you're utterly fed up with the outdated ideas surrounding work (Think: Workplace fulfillment is only for the special chosen few). Maybe you are willing to play a key role in smashing this widespread view—and many other destructive views about workplace life—into tiny pieces. If so, I'm glad you're here.

But I'm not naive about this, and I don't want you to be, either. The challenge of making our workplaces work is going to be *hard work.*

Allow me to give you a very real example of what you may be up against if you choose to accept this challenge of positively transforming the workplace.

THE CONFERENCE CONFRONTATION

Even though the following situation happened to me over four years ago, and it lasted fewer than seven minutes or so, I still remember it vividly. Specifically, I'll never forget the look of pure, unfiltered disgust that was in this complete stranger's eyes as she locked her eyes on mine. We both stared at each other in an awkward, prolonged silence before she finally cut through the icy pause by aiming a simple, and very blunt, rhetorical question directly at me. "Wow, you really don't get it, do you?"

I'm sure that we both had that thought simultaneously at that point, but the woman I was speaking with beat me to the punch by saying it first. She was a smartly dressed woman in her early fifties, who was tall, attractive, and just oozed power and influence, as if she had been plucked from Central Casting to star in an executive role at a top health insurance company.

We had met a few minutes earlier at a professional conference, and after discovering that she actually did hold an executive position at a top health insurance company, our run-of-the mill networking small talk took an interesting turn when we started talking about the issues facing the modern workplace.

She spoke first.

> *"I believe that the biggest issue is that it's damn near impossible to find good, hardworking, and reliable people to do front line work these days. Most of these people are lazy, entitled, spoiled, millennial brats who feel that they should be given a trophy whenever they show up to work on time. Poorly trained and incompetent front line employees cost organizations millions of dollars a year in lost productivity, and we need to put a stop to it. There's no doubt in my mind that if we can find a way to just fix these people, we could improve the workplace significantly."*

[Cue my eye twitching uncontrollably as I tried to mask my raging frustration.] Did she really just say "fix" these people?

As a corporate trainer and consultant, I have heard variations of the same tired spiel more times than I care to admit, and it still kills a tiny piece of my soul each time.

Here we go again, I thought. Another high-ranking, out-of-touch corporate suit who was quick to back the bus over the men and women whose hard work was allowing her to rock the Prada purse hanging from her shoulder. Equally as troubling to me was that her solution would only treat a symptom of the workplace illness that is negatively affecting millions of people all over the world.

I'm trying to provide the cure.

She seemed pretty passionate about her stance, so that's why I paused for a moment when she asked for my opinion on the issue. I have dealt with many people like this woman throughout my career, so I already knew that she was going to despise my response as soon as I opened my mouth. But since I figured that she was the type of person who could benefit from hearing it the most, I happily shared my solution with her anyway:

"I believe that the biggest issue facing the modern workplace is that we desperately need more positivity."

As predicted, the imaginary needle on the record *screeched* loudly off the turntable.

After looking at me as if I had sprouted a third eyeball in the center of my forehead, she instantly switched from a state of confusion into attack mode, and responded with a flurry of disbelief, disgust, and annoyance that I will never forget as long as I live.

"Positivity? Are you kidding?! Look, I've been in the business world for a long time and it will take a lot more than dreaming about sunshine, rainbows, and kittens to fix the issues facing the workplace. If you think that we can fix the workplace by opening up a 'Free Hugs' booth at the front door of every company on this earth, then you are completely delusional. It will take real, meaningful work to fix the issues in the workplace."

Still smiling, but admittedly annoyed at this point, I looked her in the eyes and flatly responded, "Right. We're actually talking about the exact same thing. Positivity *is* the real work."

That's when she paused, shook her head in disbelief at my naiveté, and with a condescending chuckle informed me that I "don't get it" before she rolled her eyes and walked away in hopes of finding a more like-minded discussion partner.

Sigh. Yes, this is exactly what we're up against.

Here's the real twist to this story: I could empathize with every disgusted eye roll, passive-aggressive smirk, and dismissive head shake that she fired in my direction.

Positivity, as most people think of it, is a complete joke. For many people, the joke becomes even more ridiculous and laughable when people talk about it as a tool to improve the modern workplace.

Dreaming about sunshine, rainbows, and kittens? You have to admit, that's pretty funny.

But it's also stupid.

Even worse, it's dangerous. Especially since it has nothing to do with what real positivity is all about. That's why I need to start by setting the record straight once and for all.

I will give that lady props on one point, though: Opening up a "Free Hugs" booth at the entrance of every company will *not* solve the issues facing the modern workplace.

Thankfully, I know what will.

POSITIVITY, REIMAGINED

Do I have your permission to keep it brutally real? Excellent. Here goes:

The state of the American workplace is a mess. It's not even a hot one, either.

Recent studies show that over two-thirds of those in the U.S. workforce[1] are either sleepwalking through their workdays as unengaged, soulless zombies or they are actively disengaged and spreading misery, negativity, and discontent to whomever they come in contact with. Even worse, these people cost the United States anywhere from $450 to $550 billion each year in lost productivity.[2] To put that in perspective, with that amount of money you could buy *every* professional sports team in *every* professional sports league in the United States, with many billions left to spare.

Wait, there's more. A mind-boggling 65 million Americans are currently affected by the blight of workplace bullying.[3] As you are reading these words, many of those people are struggling to deal with an unwelcome reality: Life-altering health issues, ranging from hypertension to post-traumatic stress disorder, are their constant companions. Employees are unappreciated, treated rudely, and dehumanized by their colleagues, customers, and bosses more than ever before. This is the sad—and inarguably broken—state of the modern workplace for millions of people all over the world (more on this later).

So, how are we going to solve all of this? Simple. We need to start by rebuilding our workplaces from a new and unshakable foundation.

Positivity.

Before we move forward, though, let's make sure that we're all on the same page with what I mean by positivity.

The word *positive* is officially defined by Merriam-Webster as "showing progress, gain, or improvement," and the word *positivity* is officially defined as "the state of being positive." To me, those official definitions are an excellent start, but they're missing *how* to show progress, gain, or improvement in the workplace.

So, here's the official definition of *positivity* that I'll be working from:

> ***The act of consistently using kindness and mutual respect to create improved outcomes.***

No, this has nothing to do with optimism (although I'm a die-hard optimist myself), deluding ourselves into believing that things are great when they clearly are not, or high-fiving and fist-bumping any human being who comes within five feet of us. This is about creating improved outcomes at work by consistently treating each other with kindness and mutual respect. That's it.

It doesn't matter if you are part of a flight crew for a commercial airline, a paralegal at a busy law firm, a charge nurse for a cardiac unit in a hospital, a call-center agent for an insurance company, an elementary school teacher, or the person working the drive-through window at a fast food restaurant. A culture of positivity, as it is defined here, will create improved outcomes in any workplace environment.

Why kindness and mutual respect?

After years of research and a decade of personally training and coaching thousands of men and women of every title, race, age, and background in various industries, there were only two recurring workplace themes that were painfully lacking on low-performing teams and abundant on high-performing teams: kindness and mutual respect.

The definitions of both are clear and easy to follow. *Kindness* is displaying a benevolent and helpful nature toward others. *Mutual respect* is mutually caring about each other's feelings and well-being.

Simple, isn't it?

So here is where we must begin. This consistent lack of kindness and respect is the primary obstacle keeping many individuals, departments, and organizations from showing the progress, gain, or improvement that they desperately crave.

This issue has been ignored, laughed off, and dismissed for way too long, and we can no longer afford to wait for the imaginary "someone else" to come save us and our workplaces. It's time for us to forge a movement of people who will finally address it directly.

Yes, you read that correctly: *By creating a workplace movement around positivity, we will finally make our workplaces work.*

The good news is that the special group of people who have the guts, intelligence, and passion to make this movement a reality actually exist.

And no, it's not the lady at the conference, or others like her, who are going to be the ones to make it happen. They are the ones who created this mess in the first place.

We will need to look elsewhere, and there is one place where we'll need to start.

The mirror.

It doesn't matter if you're eighteen years old or sixty-five years old. Your job title doesn't matter, either. The only thing that matters is if you are surrounded by jerks and/or negativity in your workplace. If so, and you deeply desire to do something to change it, then the person in your mirror can save you.

This book is written to show that person exactly how to do it.

If you're still not convinced, that's okay—I didn't expect this to be an easy sell. It's certainly possible that you've been led to believe some very destructive myths about positivity and, more specifically, about your ability to make positive change in your workplace.

Let's start here by putting these myths to bed for good.

FROM MYTH TO REALITY: SETTING THE RECORD STRAIGHT

There are countless myths about positivity at work, so without further ado, let's attack five of the most common ones that you might believe.

Myth #1:

Seriously? A positivity movement at work? Good luck getting people onboard with that silliness. It will never work.

Yes, it will.

There are literally millions of people in the world who are desperate to be free from a lifetime of misery, debilitating stress, and hopelessness in their jobs. You might be one of them.

If so, isn't it time to do something about this? I mean, *really* do something about this? No, I'm not talking about overthrowing the jerks, bullies, and negative people in your workplace (well . . . not initially, anyway). This is about organizing as many people as possible around one simple and powerful idea: consistently using kindness and mutual respect to create improved outcomes at work.

All this movement needs is one person to get it started. Just one. Once one person is fed up enough to do the hard work to transform the workplace into the positive environment that it should have been from the start, the movement begins. Once that person makes that courageous stand, that act will serve as an invitation for others to join in and make their stamp on history. The real question is this: Is that person you?

At its core, this movement is about leading by example to create a culture of positivity in the workplace. Be forewarned: This is not for the faint of heart. This book will reveal the shared actions we will need to take to ensure that this movement does not merely survive, but thrive. This book will reveal how to make this movement grow and flourish. No more waiting for our Human Resources Departments or another employee-satisfaction survey to save us from this mess. We need to claim our positive work experience. Today. Or, better yet, right now.

Sound impossible?

At one time, the thought of running a mile in under four minutes was considered impossible. But on May 6, 1954, a man named Roger Bannister proved otherwise by becoming the first human being to run a mile in less than four minutes. Since his successful stand against the impossible, he inspired a movement of speed demons (including kids in high school!) who have successfully done the impossible by running sub-four-minute miles. Did human beings magically become faster runners on May 6, 1954, or did they just need someone to show them that what was once widely considered impossible wasn't impossible at all?

I think you know the answer.

There was a time when many considered the elimination of the deep-seated racial segregation in America to be impossible. Martin Luther King, Jr. thought differently about the issue, and he inspired a movement of people to believe in his dream of a new America, too. As a result of his passion and his focus on a singular goal, he played a major role in inspiring Congress to pass the Civil Rights Act of 1964, which made racial discrimination illegal in America. One man's courage and vision for a better future served as the spark to move an entire nation in a positive direction. Many thought that his dream was impossible, but once the movement gained momentum, there was no stopping it from reaching its desired end.

The examples of people making the impossible possible are too numerous to list here, but I want you to rethink what is truly possible for you and for me. Allowing the enormity of the task ahead of us to stop us before we start carries significant consequences. Too many people are hurting from working in toxic work environments, and it would be immoral for us to turn a blind eye to it any longer. Together we can launch this movement and use our collective passion for workplace positivity to effectively change our lives, our departments, and, quite possibly, the world.

Myth #2:

Okay, I'll go along with the mutual respect part—but making kindness the foundation of your workplace positivity movement is an absolute joke. Sometimes you need to kick people in the ass to get things done. That's how you make a workplace work. Leaders need to lead, baby.

This is just silly. The real joke is the tired idea that a person can't be kind and still be a leader. This is not an either/or type of deal.

A person can consistently hold people accountable for their actions and still be kind. A person can kick people in the ass (*figuratively*, in case you had any ideas) and still be kind. A person can be a strong leader and still be kind.

That's because true kindness requires strength and conviction. Case in point:

Let's say that there is an employee named Susie who is consistently rude to her customers, is regularly late to work, and spreads vicious lies about her colleagues to anyone who will listen.

Do you think that the kind way to get her to shape up is by relentlessly hugging her, showering her with gift cards and thank-you notes, and softly singing some show tunes in her ear until she succumbs to your positive vibes and magically becomes a better employee? If so, let me know how that worked out for you after your inevitable appointment with your Human Resources office (or with the police).

You might laugh but, sadly, there are people out there who cling to an even more ridiculous idea of "kindness at work" than what you just read.

The reality is that holding people accountable *is* an act of kindness, it is an act of strength and conviction, and it is certainly an act of positivity, too. If anything, allowing Susie's behavior to continue unchecked may be one of the most unkind, negative, and destructive things you could do for her, her colleagues, and her customers. Positivity is about improving outcomes and, in Susie's case, this goal can be met by holding her to a higher standard in a firm, direct, and respectful way.

The misguided idea that the only way to improve Susie's behavior is to yell at, intimidate, and demean her is about as fresh and modern as lava lamps, horse-drawn buggies, and the stegosaurus.

Times have changed, and how to effectively lead others has changed as well. The myth that you cannot effectively lead others while being kind is officially dead. Kindness is *not* weakness. However, the same can't be said for the leader who loses his cool the minute something does not go according to plan.

Leaders do need to lead—that should go without saying. It's how they do it that matters.

Myth #3:

Positivity is all about ignoring the negative (or less-than-positive) things that are happening around us.

In a word, no.

This is without question the most frustrating myth surrounding positivity. I'm not sure where it came from, but there is a pesky view that positive people are the village idiots of the world, walking around with perma-grins plastered on their catatonic faces, too tipsy from the toxic Positivity potion they've been chugging to notice the changes in the world around them.

Let's be honest—I don't know anyone like the person just described, and I doubt that you do, either.

There is nothing positive about sticking your fingers in your ears and yelling, "I can't hear you! I'm going to keep it positive! La, la, laaaaaaaaaa!" when your boss is trying to give you some difficult feedback about your job performance.

There's nothing positive about pressing the DELETE button on all your customer complaint emails—unless your goals are to get fired, to create an army of pissed-off customers who are plotting to slash your tires at the first opportunity, or to put your company out of business.

Most of all, there's nothing positive about ignoring how your job is killing your soul, because that is the most direct path to a life-shortening nervous breakdown I have ever known.

None of these behaviors are even in the same galaxy as the positivity needed for this movement. But you already knew that.

The reason this myth is so frustrating to me is that I believe this myth is kept alive by the miserable people of the world who lack the guts, willingness, and emotional resilience to think positively. Instead, they have created ridiculous, over-the-top, and completely fictional caricatures of positive people so that they won't have to do the real work of creating improved outcomes in the workplace for themselves and others.

On the other hand, bringing a steady stream of negativity to the workplace is not only *way* too easy, but also it created the situation that this book has been written to solve. So to the negative people . . . thanks, I guess?

As mentioned earlier, positivity is all about taking action to create improved outcomes by being consistently kind and respectful.

It's impossible to do that if our heads are stuck in the sand, ignoring reality.

Myth #4:

This is just another lame excuse for employees to cling to so they can avoid having to work hard.

At one of my recent speaking engagements, there was a very fired-up gentleman in the audience who was not feeling the urge to jump on the positivity train, to put it mildly. During the question-and-answer session, he stood up and started to get red-faced and visibly angry as he unleashed a verbal diatribe against the concept of positivity in the workplace. Since I'm sure that there may be other people who feel the same way as that gentleman, I had to formally add this myth to the list. Here's what he said:

"No offense but all of this crap is a perfect example of the wussification of America. I can see it now—employees all over the country now have a built-in excuse not to work hard because they can claim that their work environment wasn't 'positive enough' for them to do so. It's pathetic. The workplace doesn't need more positivity. It needs more people who are willing to work hard!"

At a quick glance, it sounds like he's on point, doesn't it? Unfortunately, his argument is missing one key element. I'll use a quick analogy to explain.

Let's say that I try to relive my long-lost glory days at the local basketball court this afternoon and I end up breaking my leg in the process. A few days later, I'm at home propped up in my bed with a cast on my leg, and in an attempt to help me recover from my injury, you decide to show up at my house with an electric saw in your hand.

Uh-oh. This can't be good.

You shrug off my look of pure terror as you coolly say, "Look, man, the only way your leg is going to get better is if you learn how to walk on it again. Put on your big boy britches—I'm going to saw your cast off and you're going to walk. Now."

First of all, I would probably call the cops on your crazy ass, because remember, *my leg is broken.* And if you somehow convinced me to follow your insane treatment plan, it would likely do me and my leg infinitely more harm than good. And that's exactly the problem.

Many of our workplaces are severely broken, too—in some extreme cases, irreparably so. Painting a fresh coat of hard work over the rotten and broken lumber that's serving as the current foundation of our workplaces isn't going to solve anything, any more than trying to walk on a freshly broken leg would.

As we already noted, people are miserable at work. Telling these people that the solution to their workplace problems is to just buck up and work harder is insulting and totally off the mark.

We need to start the healing process by building a solid foundation first. Thinking that people will work their hardest and produce at their maximum capacity in a toxic work environment just isn't realistic, sensible, or effective anymore. And it never was.

Focusing on creating an environment of kindness, mutual respect, and positivity is how we must start if we're trying to heal our broken workplaces. This is deeper than hard work for hard work's sake. This is about the thoughtful practice of making our workplaces work, for our future's sake.

Myth #5:

The modern workplace is too broken to be fixed, especially by positivity.

I might be the only person alive who believes that this is a myth, and I'm okay with being the crazy guy who believes that an age-old issue can be fixed by a simple idea.

I know that fixing the modern workplace and making it a more positive experience for millions of people all over the world is going to take an enormous amount of effort, but didn't we already know that? The real question is this: Can we afford to allow the enormity of the task to scare us away from doing the necessary work any longer?

Speaking of scary, there is nothing scarier than the future if we choose do nothing about this.

Millions of people are living in complete misery at work as you're reading these words. Even if you're not one of those people (yet), I'd be willing to guess that misery at work is likely affecting a loved one or a friend of yours. And even if that's not the case, there's no doubt that you will eventually cross paths with someone whose life has taken a turn to the dark side, due largely to how she is treated at work.

It could be a disengaged food service employee—yes, the one who will be handling your lunch later on today—who doesn't care enough to wash his hands after he uses the restroom. It could be a disengaged nurse charged with giving you the proper dose of medication at the hospital, but she's too broken, beaten down, and distracted to do it correctly. Or it could be a disengaged teacher who is entrusted with helping prepare your child for college one day, but instead, has resigned himself to giving his school and his students the least possible effort to keep him from getting fired.

Are you willing to live with these risks?

This is too important to be ignored for a minute longer because this is hurting, or will hurt, too many people—including you or someone you love.

Most people don't become miserable or disengaged in their jobs because they dislike the work they're doing—it's because they dislike the people they're doing the work with. The goal of this movement is to address that stubborn issue once and for all, and I believe that we (yes, *we*) have everything that we need within us to fix the broken state of the American workplace.

But only if we are willing to do the work.

Nelson Mandela said it best: "It always seems impossible until it's done."

We can do the impossible, and it's time to address why we cannot wait a moment longer to do it.

CHAPTER

2

WAITING FOR HAPPINESS

The Insanity of Inaction

You can dance in the storm. Don't wait for the rain to be over
because it might take too long. You can do it now.
Wherever you are, you can start, right now; this very moment.

—ISRAELMORE AYIVOR

This is going to sound a little strange, but humor me for a minute. I want you to imagine that there's a hideous green-skinned, pointy-eared, red-eyed alien from the planet Elohssa who is running around unchecked in your workplace—let's call him Krej.

Unlike most aliens who specialize in abducting humans and appearing in bad sci-fi movies, Krej likes to cause all sorts of mischief and drama in workplaces all over the earth. Worst of all, Krej has a dark and very evil superpower:

He can cause any career that he touches to die a slow death.

Recently, two brilliant women heard about the legend of Krej and decided to observe this little monster in action to see how destructive he really is around the workplace. What they found after observing this mischievous creature was horrifying:

- 12 percent of employees said they left their job because of him.
- 25 percent of employees said they took their frustrations out on their customers after they dealt with him.

- 38 percent of employees said they intentionally decreased the quality of their work after dealing with him.
- 48 percent of employees intentionally decreased their work effort after dealing with him.
- 66 percent of employees said that their performance declined because of him.
- 78 percent of employees said that their commitment to the organization declined because of him.[1]

Clearly, this is a big problem.

Hold on, it actually gets worse: *Krej has the ability to multiply himself.*

In fact, Krej has clones of himself everywhere. Every workplace from the high-profile accounting firm all the way to the cookie store in the mall food court has to deal with this nuisance destroying everything of importance inside every place of employment on earth—including yours. This alien is an absolute menace.

Based on what you've heard so far, let me ask you a few questions.

Do you think that Krej is an enemy that should be underestimated, dismissed, or ignored?

Do you think there's a company anywhere on earth that should do anything short of calling in nuclear-armed military forces to prevent this alien from coming within one hundred miles of its front door?

Is there any priority that's more urgent than systematically killing a threat that has the power to make a large proportion of employees lazy, bitter, uncommitted to their company, and willing to lash out at their customers at a moment's notice?

You've answered no to all of the above, right? Perfect. So far, so good.

Here's where it gets weird, though (as if talking about an alien named "Krej" wasn't weird enough). Very few organizations are committed to killing off this threat. In fact, many organizations turn a blind eye to Krej's presence, helplessly shrug their shoulders when they see him roaming the hallways of their companies, and, in many cases, accept him (yes, accept him!) as part of the company culture.

As a result, Krej has made, and will continue to make, workplaces all over the world nearly unbearable because very few people have the courage or the willingness to talk about—or, better yet, *deal with*—the green, pointy-eared alien in the room.

This, my friend, is the insanity of inaction. And to reclaim our workplaces from this monster, it's time for us to fully wake up and understand the enemy we're up against so we can collectively get sane.

Quickly.

THE NEW ENEMY OF POSITIVITY, REVEALED

To no one's surprise, this is not about an alien named "Krej," but it's specifically about the very real problem that Krej represents. From now on, let's refer to this irritating alien by his given name: Workplace Incivility.

Now he sounds more familiar, doesn't he? I know you have met this alien before. If you're still not familiar with Krej, just spell the alien's name backward (or better yet, spell the planet he's from backward) and I'm sure you'll recognize him.

Before we dive more deeply into the madness, let's clearly define what we're up against.

Professors Christine Pearson and Christine Porath, in their book *The Cost of Bad Behavior*, define workplace incivility as follows:

> *"the exchange of seemingly inconsequential inconsiderate words and deeds that violate conventional norms of workplace conduct."*[2] *In other words, workplace incivility is the consistent rudeness, thoughtlessness, and passive-aggressiveness that sucks the life out of you and makes you question your faith in humanity.*

No, we're not talking about the extreme stuff, like workplace bullying—we'll get to that soul-crushing awfulness later on. It's the day-to-day rudeness that has the power to slowly chip away at our drive, our passion, and our overall professional effectiveness.

Here are some, but definitely not all, common examples of it:

- Belittling a colleague, the work done by a colleague, or both
- Spreading rumors or gossiping about others
- Practicing poor email etiquette, such as sending an email without a greeting, using all caps, unnecessarily (and passive-aggressively) cc-ing the entire leadership team on every email
- Purposely failing to acknowledge a "Hello" or "Good morning"
- Ignoring employees' concerns, thoughts, or input
- Not cleaning up after yourself, or, alternatively, expecting others to clean up your messes
- Stealing or "forgetting" to share credit for a job well done
- Flaking out on scheduled meetings, being consistently late, or purposely keeping people waiting
- Casting the blame on others for your own mistakes
- Failing to say "Please," "Thank you," "I'm sorry," or "Excuse me"
- Coming into work sick and spreading your germs to others
- Eye rolling, loud sighing, head-shaking, and the like when someone is talking
- Interrupting, not listening
- Withholding information
- Criticizing people in front of others
- Swiping through your cell phone or otherwise not paying attention during a meeting
- Yelling or raising your voice

I know what some people might be thinking.

"Wow, have we gotten so soft as a society that people can't recover from someone failing to acknowledge a 'Good morning' greeting? Do people need a therapist on standby to help them cope with the indignity of receiving an email that doesn't address them by name?! Good Lord, are you people listening to yourselves?!"

Whatever you do, please don't be that person.

It's time to reject emotionally absent, meathead, pseudo–tough guy/girl silliness, and realize that being on the business end of repeated and consistent rudeness and incivility hurts. A lot. And it's not just the recipient of the incivility who feels the pain. So does the company he works for.

Professors Pearson and Porath detailed the consequences of allowing this behavior to continue unchecked during their ten-plus years of research on workplace incivility. The data specified earlier in this chapter, in connection with "Krej," should serve as an ear-piercing wake-up call to all employers about the damage that workplace civility can cause to any organization. It would be unwise and irresponsible for any organization to ignore it for another day.

On the flip side, there is an enormous benefit that can come from finding the courage to deal directly with the people who are making our workplaces miserable with their ongoing rudeness and incivility. I have seen departments break into celebrations reminiscent of children on the last day of school when disruptively rude employees have either quit or were let go from their jobs. That is an excellent example of addition by subtraction, and its effect has the power to positively transform a work team overnight.

So is this about firing all the rude people in your company? If it were only that simple. But no, that's not what I'm talking about. This is specifically about creating workplace cultures that would make it very difficult—if not impossible—for these people to grow and flourish. It is also about providing us with the tools and strategies to push forward despite the people who will try to slow down this movement.

Is there any other option that makes sense? Haven't we ignored this issue for long enough? How many more billions of dollars need to be flushed down the drain each year before we do something? How many millions of U.S. citizens need to be crushed emotionally and mentally before we quit sleepwalking and focus all our collective efforts on solving this issue?

One thing is for sure—inaction is not the solution you're looking for.

There's another thing that won't provide any meaningful solutions, either.

HEY, IT IS WHAT IT IS: EXCUSING THE OFFICE JERKS

You have heard all these excuses before, I'm sure.

"Learn to deal with it."

"It's part of the gig, man."

"It could be worse."

"Feel lucky that you have a job."

"It is what it is."

Enough. I'm done with the excuses and I hope you are, too.

Of all the barriers, obstacles, and roadblocks that get in the way of creating a culture of workplace positivity, this is the one that keeps hanging around like an ex-boyfriend or an ex-girlfriend who can't take a hint. No more.

There's no excuse for allowing a consistent culture of rudeness and incivility to exist in your workplace if you have any interest in maintaining your sanity and/or working on a high-functioning team. Here are three reasons why.

1. Excuses can destroy your career.

Horrifying workplace incivility statistic: Studies have shown that 78 percent of employees and managers decrease their commitment to an organization due to workplace incivility.

Although this statistic was presented earlier in reference to Krej, I'd like to add my own personal example to the mix.

I used to work for a woman who was the queen of incivility. Depending on where the bouncing ball landed on her roulette wheel of extreme moods, it would determine whether or not my coworkers and I were in for a bearable day. Maybe you can personally relate to this.

She would regularly criticize us in front of colleagues and customers, she would keep us waiting for thirty to sixty minutes for scheduled meetings because she was too busy gossiping with the other managers on the floor to honor our meeting times, she would interrupt us mid-sentence, talk over us, and roll her eyes and loudly sigh whenever we said anything that she didn't agree with. Most annoying of all, she would show exceptional kindness to her peers, her superiors, and her customers, but for some reason, she was incapable of extending the same kindness to us.

After three years of dealing with this, I decided to finally take matters into my own hands. Like most people dealing with workplace rudeness, I didn't feel comfortable bringing my issues to the Human Resources Department. I don't think that reporting that "My boss is moody, interrupts us all the time, and acts like she's better than us" would make it to the top of any HR representative's priority list.

So instead, I decided to raise my concerns to her boss. Here's the lame response that I received in return:

"She's passionate. She just wants what's best for the organization."

Passionate, huh? Let's dig more deeply into this.

Her passion prompted four highly skilled people to quit in less than three years and find jobs with a major competitor. Two of those people needed to undergo weekly therapy just to deal with the challenge of being in her presence for forty hours a week. There was not one of us, myself included, who was not actively looking for another job while she was in charge. Worst of all, a team of exemplary professionals consistently questioned their skills, career choice, and sanity, due in large part to how rudely she treated them on a daily basis.

Personally speaking, the thought of dealing with my former boss each day weighed on my mind like a seventy-five-pound boat anchor. Even though I wouldn't classify her as a workplace bully, the negative effects of our repeated interactions extended far beyond the workplace. Over time, I felt myself change in ways that deeply troubled me. I struggled to sleep through the night, I noticed myself behaving just as rudely as she did (something I vowed I would never do), and, worst of all, many of my closest personal relationships were adversely affected. Looking back on it now, those were some of the worst years of my professional life, and many of my former colleagues who went through it with me feel the exact same way.

Contrary to popular belief, it doesn't always take being stabbed through the heart by the blade of workplace bullying to negatively affect a career. Sometimes, receiving ten thousand paper cuts from the page of incivility can have the same destructive effect.

2. Excuses can kill you.

Horrifying workplace incivility statistics: A survey of healthcare professionals revealed that 67 percent of them felt that there was a linkage between disruptive behaviors and adverse events, 71 percent felt there was a linkage to medical errors, and 27 percent felt that there was a linkage to patient mortality.[3]

If those statistics don't scare the hell out of you, then I am sincerely in awe of your fearlessness. For the rest of us, let's meet a nurse whose story exemplifies the dangers of incivility in a health-care setting.

> *Janice was a nurse at a large and well-respected hospital on the east coast. For close to two years, Janice dealt with a physician who would consistently talk to her and her nurse colleagues in a condescending manner whenever they fell short of clairvoyance and did not anticipate his next move. Go-to behaviors from his interpersonal bag of horrors included dismissively rolling his eyes when they would speak, slamming his fist on the table whenever he was frustrated with the nurses' performance, verbally shaming the nurses whenever he was on call and the nurses actually called him (imagine that), and demanding that they become proficient in reading his mind.*

Janice and two of her nurse colleagues decided that they were fed up with this guy's intolerable behavior and brought this concern directly to the hospital administration. Here's what they received for their trouble:

"He's such a gifted and brilliant physician. He's not going to change, so you're going to have to learn how to communicate with him."

Unfortunately, that didn't cut it for Janice. The nurses continued to work in fear of him as they walked on eggshells around him on a daily basis, but Janice couldn't do it. She admitted that his treatment of her undermined her ability to provide quality patient care because she felt constantly distracted, on edge, and unsafe as a result of his behavior. She even admitted to making errors that affected patient safety, which isn't surprising considering the statistic mentioned earlier.

Here's the question that every responsible professional must consider: Are we willing to risk a human life because we're too enamored of our silly excuses to directly confront the green-skinned, red-eyed alien in the room—regardless of how much influence and prestige that alien has going for him?

While I can't speak for anyone else in the nursing profession, Janice was one of those nurses who refused to deal with having the inexcusable being excused whenever *MD* followed the perpetrator's name. After having her faith in humanity pushed past the limit on a daily basis, she made the very difficult decision to walk away from her lifelong dream and quit. These days, Janice is allowing her considerable nursing skills to collect dust while she works in another field completely unrelated to health care.

In this story, everyone loses.

According to the former colleagues Janice left behind, the hospital leadership is still using the physician's brilliance (or, more honestly—the fear that he would take his sizable patient load with him if he ever left) as an excuse to look the other way.

Hopefully, it won't take someone dying unnecessarily before the hospital leaders decide to take this issue seriously, but I wouldn't be surprised at all if it did.

3. Excuses can drive away business.

Horrifying workplace incivility statistic: According to a recent *Harvard Business Review* study, customers who witnessed employees being rude to each other were four times more likely to walk away from the company.[4]

Mark is a retail employee at a clothing store in the mall. His colleague Javier is one of the longest-tenured employees at the store, and he is known for his boorish and unfriendly behavior. When he arrives on shift, he greets no one, makes snide comments about the clothing not being folded in the correct manner, and often blames his fellow coworkers when customers voice a complaint.

By far, Javier's most egregious behavior is tactlessly nitpicking and criticizing his coworkers in front of customers. That has created quite a few cringe-worthy moments for the customers of the store, and many employees understandably hate working with him because of it. Even worse, some of the regular customers have even complained to Mark that they don't like Javier's rude, condescending, and unpleasant attitude, and that they even try to avoid Javier as much as his coworkers do.

Whenever Mark has tried to address this issue with Javier directly, he simply denies all wrongdoing and pretends that nothing is wrong.

One day after Javier berated him in front of another customer, Mark was at wit's end and he decided to bring the issue to the attention of their supervisor. Here was her response:

"He doesn't mean to be rude. Don't take his outbursts so personally. He means well."

He may "mean well," but that's far from doing well. According to Mark, his store isn't doing well, either. At last check, his particular store was in the bottom 20 percent in comparison to the rest of his company's stores nationwide.

It's obvious that customers don't like being treated poorly by the service staff. But what many people also fail to realize is that they don't like seeing staff members treat other staff members poorly, either.

The Worst Excuse of All

If you thought the previous excuses were bad, here's the one thing that can put all three of those excuses to shame: defending incivility.

There's a small—and potentially growing—pocket of emotional Neanderthals who have no interest in finding excuses for incivility because, to them, there is nothing to excuse. Even worse, they believe that treating others terribly is an effective way to get results. A well-known physician once told me that he longs for the "good ol' days" when he was able to blow off steam and curse at his nurses without them feeling as if they could actually do anything about it.

Scary, isn't it? He wasn't kidding, either.

For people like him, rudeness and incivility are effective motivational tools that will make the target of these barbs stronger after surviving them. It's as if these people believe that viciousness builds competence and skill. After all, how will your employees or colleagues know how much you care about them and how committed you are to a standard of excellence if you don't yell and scream at them, right?

There's an obvious problem with this strategy, though: It doesn't work. All it does is establish rudeness as the norm and create a new generation of employees who will pass on their gifts of incivility at the earliest possible moment they are able to do so.

Those gifts could end up with workers putting in minimal effort or sabotaging an important project, throwing a coworker under the bus to avoid having the boss's wrath directed at him, or feeling so pissed off by how he's being treated that he spits into an unsuspecting customer's food as a way to vent his anger, instead of confronting the issue. All these gifts are inexcusable, of course, but it's naive to think that they don't happen in environments in which incivility and rudeness rule the day.

Excusing incivility and rudeness is a convenient, and costly, diversion from rolling up our sleeves and doing the necessary work to create a culture of positivity in our workplaces.

It's time to raise the bar, reject the excuses, and recognize that inaction will only succeed in binding us more tightly to the problem we're trying to break free from.

Freedom can only come from taking action, and that action must be taken now.

You may be wondering, what's the rush?

Because Krej is not a figment of our imagination—he's very real and whether you believe in him or not, the alien invasion has already begun. And here's the kicker:

It's up to you to stop it.

Let's see if you're ready.

CHAPTER

3

THE RISE OF THE SOLUTIONISTS

The Power of Keeping It R.E.A.L.

Life is really simple, but we insist on making it complicated.

—CONFUCIUS

Let's recap.

We've discussed what positivity is in chapter 1. We've discussed why it's so important to act now in chapter 2. Now it's time to talk about *how* we'll do it. Here is the answer:

Simplicity.

Besides incivility, needless complexity is also killing workplaces all over the world and getting in the way of making our workplaces work.

Where has complexity gotten us? The fishbone diagrams, fresh and shiny process improvement tools, and countless researched studies have left us pretty much where we started at the beginning of this mess: *Americans still hate their jobs.*

The problem is that many people don't want to let go of the idea that the solution to our workplace issues has to be complex, painful, time-consuming, and expensive. Complexity makes us feel important, it gives us a convenient excuse when problems aren't solved, and in some cases, it's more attractive than an equally effective, simpler option.

Given the choice, if these books were side by side on a bookshelf with the exact same content inside, which one would you reach for first?

1. *The Hollywood Body Secret: The Proven and Timeless Techiques to Look and Feel Like an A-Lister Every Day*

2. *The Do-It-Now Plan: Stop Eating Crap and Start Working Out*

I don't know many people who would reach for the second book, because it's way too simple, and besides, we already know that. But it works. Ask any dietitian.

Simple things work.

We're facing the same challenge here. I believe that we can change the world at work if we simply commit to treating each other better. Simple? Absolutely. *But it works.* Ask any of the millions of employees all over the world who are currently on the receiving end of hideous treatment at the workplace.

I'll even take this simplicity idea one step further.

How do you feel about this?

> *You, and every person who you are currently working with, are either part of the problem or part of the solution when it comes to making the workplace better for your colleagues and customers.*

There is no need to overcomplicate this because there are no exceptions.

And to simplify this still further, I have a quiz for you. It's called the "Are You Making Work Work? Quiz" and it is made up of thirty-two True/False questions to determine which side of the Positivity Line (problem or solution) you are currently on. All you have to do is answer each question as honestly as you can.

Don't agonize over each question, either—just answer with whatever pops into your mind after you read it: "True" or "False."

This is the first step in determining your readiness to become an active participant in this movement and to finally make our workplaces work. The ones who are ready for this movement will be affectionately known as *Solutionists.* In a world full of problem pointers (aka, people who point out problems and do nothing else), Solutionists are the ones who are focused on being problem solvers and living each day as part of the solution in their professional and personal lives.

The world needs more Solutionists, and it is time to see if you are ready to become one.

Good luck.

ARE YOU MAKING WORK WORK? QUIZ:

This quiz is a two-part process, and the first part simply calls for you to answer "True" or "False" in response to the following questions and score your results.

Part 1

1. Creating a workplace culture of kindness and mutual respect is a silly and unrealistic goal. **T** or **F**
2. Whenever I hear employees making small talk that's not work-related, that's a cue that they don't have enough work to do. **T** or **F**
3. I usually don't apologize for hurting someone's feelings—whether I did it intentionally or unintentionally. **T** or **F**
4. I prefer to talk *about* people than to talk *to* people. **T** or **F**
5. When I'm stressed out (due to a fast-approaching deadline, a bad mood, or for any other reason), I am a very difficult person to be around. **T** or **F**
6. I expect colleagues to be available to address work-related issues via email, text, or cell phone during off hours, weekends, and even while they're on vacation. **T** or **F**
7. *Workplace bullying* has turned into a catchphrase for overly sensitive people who can't handle constructive criticism, accountability, or hard work. **T** or **F**
8. The ability to use fear to your advantage is a critical skill that should be in the tool kit of every effective leader. **T** or **F**
9. I have been told by multiple people that I have an attitude problem and/or that I am unapproachable. **T** or **F**
10. Thanking your employees or colleagues too often will make them complacent and unwilling to work hard. **T** or **F**
11. If you disrespect me, you can count on me giving you the same disrespect (if not, worse) in return. **T** or **F**

12. I have been known to complain about issues without offering solutions. **T** or **F**

13. There are perfectly legitimate reasons to yell at a colleague at work. **T** or **F**

14. In order to get any respect from me, you will need to earn it first. **T** or **F**

15. When someone at work takes advantage of me (for example, by stealing credit for my work, dumping extra work on me, or expecting me to cover for her, even though she wouldn't do the same for me), I regularly accept it and suffer in silence. **T** or **F**

16. The workplace is not a place to make friends. **T** or **F**

17. People who frequently use their vacation time are not team players and do not have their professional priorities straight. **T** or **F**

18. The reason why my work environment is awful is because of everyone else here—I have nothing to do with this mess. **T** or **F**

19. I lose my temper easily. **T** or **F**

20. Vulnerability and transparency are invitations not to be taken seriously as a leader. **T** or **F**

21. Receiving a regular paycheck from a company and the feeling of a job well done are all the recognition that any mature professional should ever need. **T** or **F**

22. Some job roles (such as manager or director) are more important than other job roles (like janitor or administrative assistant). **T** or **F**

23. Giving feedback, coaching, and focusing on the interpersonal side of employees are low-priority pursuits that get in the way of doing the real work. **T** or **F**

24. I haven't sincerely, specifically, and meaningfully thanked a coworker in the past workweek. **T** or **F**

25. The need to be positively recognized by others in order to stay motivated is a sign of immaturity. **T** or **F**

26. I am more concerned with pleasing the people who can directly help my career (that is, my boss, my customers, my senior leaders) than I am with pleasing people who have little impact on my career success (such as my coworkers and those who report directly to me). **T** or **F**

27. You can only be a real leader at work if you have the title to back it up. **T** or **F**

28. Sometimes I'm too busy to say "Please," "Thank you," or "Excuse me." **T** or **F**

29. If I need to criticize someone's work, I have no problem doing it in front of his coworkers or customers. **T** or **F**

30. There is nothing that one person can do to positively change his or her workplace in a meaningful way. **T** or **F**

31. I rarely admit to others that I am wrong. **T** or **F**

32. I have raised my voice at someone at work in the past workweek. **T** or **F**

ANSWER KEY

0–4 True: You are officially ready to make the workplace work! Keep reading, because you clearly "get it." Or you're lying. Since I'm an optimist, I'm going with the former. Make sure to stick around because, as you'll soon see, I'm going to need your help to make this movement happen. Big time.

5–9 True: Okay, you have *some* jerklike tendencies, but you're not part of the problem that we need to deal with (not yet, anyway). I'm keeping my eye on you, though.

THE POSITIVITY LINE

10–25 True: You are officially part of the problem. Good news, though: If you are open to changing, I'm writing this book to help you. If you're not open to changing, just know that I'm writing this book and starting this movement to stop you. And *we will* stop you.

26–32 True: I'm going to appeal to your humanity for a minute. Deep down you know that these beliefs are not serving you, your colleagues, or your organization in any meaningful way. If you don't know, then here's the harsh truth: You are hurting a lot of people, and it's time to wake up to that fact before you hurt anyone else.

Part 2

Now that you've finished the self-assessment part, here's the second, and slightly harder part of the "Are You Making Work Work? Quiz."

You need to find three professional contacts and ask them to each complete the "Are You Making Work Work? Quiz" with *you* in mind. In other words, they will answer each question while thinking, *Does [insert your name] actually do the thing that's described in the question?* If they think you do, they should mark "True," if not, they should mark "False."

If two out of the three people gave you more "True" responses than you scored for yourself, that officially means you have some work to do on yourself, regardless of how you scored yourself. Identifying our blind spots and increasing our self-awareness are both critical aspects to the success of this movement.

Believe it or not, though, this quiz is just the beginning when it comes to determining your readiness to be a Solutionist. Knowing the right thing to do is fine, but do you have the necessary traits to stay true to this movement?

Let's see.

DO YOU HAVE WHAT IT TAKES?

This movement is not for everyone, so we need to determine whether or not you have what it takes to be a Solutionist. Here are the four prerequisites needed for this journey:

1. **Resilience.** What do you do when you are faced with stress, adversity, or other negative events? Do you run and hide in your shell like a turtle or rise to the challenges of life like a hero? The ability to bounce back firmly and quickly from setbacks and challenges (and there could be many) will be a necessary skill for anyone interested being a Solutionist.

2. **Persistence.** Even with the best-laid plans, we may not hit a home run on our first swing. This is going to take repeated effort, and it is easy to understand why the less dedicated

might quit early on in this journey if they don't see results overnight. Solutionists must be willing to keep showing up each day to chip away at the ice, even when it's hard to do so. *Especially* when it's hard to do so. This quality alone has the power to make or break this movement.

3. **The Ability to Connect.** We cannot positively repair our broken workplaces alone. Every Solutionist will need help, and the only way to enlist that help is to be able to effectively connect with other people. The movement cannot grow if you're the only one doing the work. It's okay to be shy or introverted—as long as you are willing to connect to others, you will be just fine.

4. **The Right Attitude.** Solutionists are not like everyone else. They don't "kinda/sorta" want to create a more positive work environment. This stuff keeps them up at night. They dream of a world in which civility and mutual respect are the unshakable norms in every workplace and are willing to go to great lengths to make that a reality. Most of all, they are not victims playing the woe-is-me card. They believe that they have what it takes right now to play a starring role in this dramatic workplace shift all over the world. This is the attitude that is needed.

Before you move forward, be honest—did you go four for four above? Three out of four of those traits won't cut it for this movement: We need a 100 percent score. If you successfully jumped over these four hurdles, let's talk about how you can use this newfound knowledge about yourself to create a culture of positivity at work.

KEEPING IT R.E.A.L. IS HOW TO MAKE OUR WORKPLACES WORK

The power of making our workplaces work lies in the idea that you have everything you need *right now* to create a culture of positivity in your workplace. Below is the simple and very straightforward four-step strategy to make it happen.

We have to keep it real. Or, more specifically, *R.E.A.L.* Through years of research, coaching, and corporate training, I discovered the four keys to making work work:

Relentless Respect

Endless Energy

Addressing the ABCs of Workplace Negativity

Lasting Leadership

Here is a brief overview of each of the four keys before we fully dive in, beginning in the next section.

The Foundation: Relentless Respect

This is where the movement must start.

In the previous chapter, we talked about the damage that incivility can wreak on an organization's overall health. In many cases, those instances of incivility could be avoided if consistent respect—or, as I like to call it, *relentless* respect—is in the forefront of every employee's mind.

This section will focus on how to positively act and communicate with each other, the importance of respecting the organization by being accountable, and how to relentlessly respect ourselves. Every. Single. Day.

This issue is a doozy, for sure. But without a foundation, there is no movement. And we need this movement, desperately. We have been fumbling around in the dark for too long, and starting today, we will finally shine a much-needed light on the situation.

The Lifeblood: Endless Energy

Everything is energy and energy is everything—literally and figuratively. Without it, we are pretty much useless—not just to everyone else but to ourselves as well. Is there anything that's worth doing or having that doesn't require energy to do well? No, because energy is defined as the capacity to do work.

Going to the gym requires energy. Chasing after your kids requires energy. Waking up in the morning requires energy. Maintaining a social life requires energy.

Do you know what else requires your energy? Your job. And, in many cases, it requires more than most people are willing or able to give. That's why we need help to maintain our energy in the workplace and manage it effectively.

The energy that we bring to our work is the blood that flows through the veins of every organization. Unfortunately, if the halls of your organization are filled with low-energy, disengaged zombies, it's as if the veins in your body had blockages that were disrupting the flow of blood to the organs that need it to survive.

This section will focus on the importance of maintaining your energy level by having the right attitude, by creating meaningful relationships that will keep you going when your energy is fading, and by liberally using the most soul-nourishing energy source in the workplace today: appreciation.

Here's the kicker: All this can be done while—wait for it—*having fun at work.*

Yeah, I said it: fun.

The Courage: Addressing the ABCs of Workplace Negativity

Every workplace has them: the Asshats who annoy you, the Bullies who intimidate you, and the Complainers who drain you. Just like a cavity that is rotting away a tooth, their decaying effect will not disappear simply by ignoring them.

To keep this movement moving forward, we will need to address the ABCs and not allow them to slow us down. This is when the journey to workplace positivity gets hard, and we will need to tap into our courage to continue moving forward.

The Spirit: Lasting Leadership

Have you ever heard the slogan, "Change: It begins with the *other person*"?

You haven't, because this slogan doesn't exist. *You* have to lead the change.

Yes, you. There is no one else who can do this, and I'm convinced that you're reading these words because you're committed to making this happen. Don't worry. I'll show you how in the following chapters, and you won't be doing this alone. But, before we get there, I have to make sure that you're locked in on two key points:

1. Creating a workplace culture of kindness, mutual respect, and positivity is how we'll finally make our workplaces work.
2. You are capable of leading the way, regardless of where you are in your career.

This is a new way of thinking in the workplace, and it will unquestionably require a new kind of leader. A leader who knows she doesn't need a title to create a culture of positivity. A leader who has the courage to create trust by leading with vulnerability and transparency. A leader who has the conviction to lead with whatever she has from wherever she is.

Do you feel like you're living an example that's worth being followed by others? Do you often wonder why we have accepted rudeness as the new normal in workplaces all over the world? Are you up for the challenge of building a movement to reclaim the workplace from the jerks who are making your life a living hell? If so, you are *exactly* who we'll need to lead the movement.

As I mentioned numerous times before, this isn't going to be easy and it's going to require some serious courage to make it happen. The opposition is fierce, it has power and influence, and it is more than ready to derail your efforts at a moment's notice.

You will face people who will say that you are a soft, immature, bleeding-heart whiner who can't handle a little criticism. You will face people who believe that demanding a culture of positivity is just an excuse for people to avoid good ol' fashioned hard work. You will face people in positions of power over you who serve as a daily reminder of the behaviors we are trying to eliminate. You will face people who believe that sincerely caring about other people is something that gets in the way of doing real work.

That is all okay—in fact, you have to be okay with it. There's a reason this problem hasn't been eradicated yet, and it's because doing so requires a group of very special leaders who are willing to do some very challenging work. My goal is to create enough leaders who will be on the right side of history by committing to creating a workplace of positivity, starting today.

The right side of history is the positive side.

The movement begins now, Solutionist. Good luck.

SECTION

2

THE FOUNDATION

Relentless Respect

CHAPTER

4

RECLAIMING YOUR EDGE

The Lie That You've Been Told (and Believed)

> Sooner or later, you're going to realize just as I did that there's a difference between knowing the path and walking the path.
>
> —MORPHEUS, *THE MATRIX*

Before we jump into this movement headfirst, I need to introduce you to four seemingly innocent words that have the power to derail this movement before it begins. Maybe you have even said these words yourself. If so, and if you care at all about positively changing the workplace, you are going to have to remove these words from your vocabulary, starting now. Ready? Here goes:

This is common sense.

Common sense is a strange thing. I'm sure that you have never met anyone who will admit to *not* having it, but I'm also sure that you have met a lot of people who clearly lack it. One thing most people can agree on when it comes to common sense is that it isn't all that common.

If it were, people would rarely, if ever, eat at fast food restaurants, they would always wash their hands after using the restroom, they would never text while driving, and they would never keep their dog locked inside a sweltering-hot car with the windows completely rolled up while they went shopping in a department store for hours.

Most people *know* not to do those things. But for some reason, many people do them anyway—even though every single one of those activities could potentially lead to their own death or the death of another innocent party.

Knowing is not good enough. It never has been. Does it really matter if someone knows that he should include leafy green veggies in his diet and exercise often if he is choosing to shovel mountains of cookie dough ice cream into his mouth while he's glued to the couch watching hours of DVR'ed television shows?

This is why common sense is so dangerous. Lots of people know what to do, but few actually do it.

I don't care about common sense and my hope is that you won't, either. It may be common sense to treat our colleagues with respect and kindness, but if everyone did it, you wouldn't be reading this book right now. The only thing that matters, and ever will matter, is *common practice.*

As Solutionists, we cannot forget the truth that most people will go to their graves failing to realize that the gap between knowing and doing is enormous. Knowing the right thing to do is nowhere close to doing the right thing, and it never has been. That is why you will never hear a person who is consistently kind and respectful say that it is common sense, because she knows how hard it is to behave that way consistently. It is the ones who are not ready to walk this path who foolishly dismiss this as common sense, while showing the world through their actions that they lack the common sense they claim to have.

Morpheus said it brilliantly to Neo in the quote at the beginning of this chapter—*there is a difference between knowing the path and walking it.* And just like Neo in *The Matrix*, we will swallow the red pill, wake up to the reality, and walk the path to reclaim our workplace edge.

WAKING UP FROM THE BIG LIE

I am familiar with the formula for life and career success.

Study hard in college, graduate from college with a degree (or two or three, if you are feeling especially studious), slap it on a resume, use all your newfound knowledge and skills to get a job, move up the corporate ladder as high as you are able or willing to climb, and success will be yours with near-mathematical certainty until you retire.

Sure, that's an oversimplified summary of a thirty-year plan, but that's pretty much the reality that most people have been sold. There's a big problem with this reality, though.

It's not the real path to success. Not even close.

College degrees and professional certifications are unquestionably an important factor in career success, but they can't do something crucial to giving you an edge in creating a positive workplace: *the ability to bring out the best in someone else.*

I'll prove it.

I want you to think of a person who brought out the absolute best in you at work—it could be your boss, a coworker, a client, or a trusted mentor. What were some of the characteristics that enabled that person to successfully bring out the best in you? In my workshops and on my blog, The Positivity Solution, I have asked thousands of people this question. Here are some of their answers:

- She consistently pushed me outside my comfort zone and challenged me to rethink what was I was capable of doing and creating. She believed in me before I was able to believe in myself.

- He accepted that mistakes are part of the learning process and never verbally destroyed me for making one. If anything, he encouraged me to recognize that making mistakes was great, as long as they were new mistakes, not old ones.

- No matter how challenging the situation with customers, he always remained calm and thoughtful and never lost his cool. While many of his peers were prone to verbal outbursts, he did the opposite. He was universally respected and well-liked, and his example is one that I have followed to this day.

- She consistently listened to me and my concerns and made me feel extremely important during my interactions with her. She wasn't swiping through her cell phone while I was talking, interrupting me, or acting as if she had something more important to do. She was always incredibly present. I loved that about her.

- She valued my contributions to the team and consistently made a point of ensuring that I felt recognized and appreciated. For the seven years that I worked for her, there was never a day when I didn't feel that I was making a meaningful difference.

- My coworker is the most encouraging person I have ever worked with. Even though he is currently dealing with some health challenges, you would never know it. He shows up to work every day with a smile on his face and is willing to support me and the team in any way possible, without complaint or excuses. It is impossible not to be a better employee, teammate, father, and person by being around him.

- My manager is fiercely loyal. She is aware of how hard we work on a daily basis, and she would never allow anyone to disparage us or disrespect us in any way. She has defended us against attacks from abusive customers, other departments, and even from senior management. She genuinely cares about us and our well-being, and my coworkers and I would run through a brick wall for her in a heartbeat if she asked.

- She is definitely a demanding boss, but she also walks the walk. There has never been a time that she has asked us to do something that she was unwilling to do herself. When things get really busy at the front desk, instead of hiding in her office, she jumps in to help without hesitation because she knows how hard we work. She has high expectations, but since she is willing to live up to those same standards, it is easier for me to do it, too.

No matter how many times I have asked this question, I have noticed two consistent themes running through all the answers: (1) a healthy respect for others is present in every interaction, and (2) there is never a mention of technical skills. *Ever.*

When you think of the person who brought out the best or worst in you, is the first thing you think of his expertise in creating pivot tables in Microsoft Excel? Is it her near-photographic mental recall of your company's policies and procedures manual? Highly unlikely.

Sure, techical skills will get us into the door at our jobs, but once we're in, we will be surrounded by a sea of people who have the same degrees and the same technical skills that we have—probably more. Our technical skills don't make us special; they make us common.

This is the lie that we have been sold:

Our technical skills are our most important professional assets.

The truth?

Our most important professional asset is the ability to bring out the best in others through our interpersonal skills.

This is the workplace edge that will separate us from the men and women we will work with throughout our careers, and that edge can only be gained through our mastery of interpersonal skills. Feel free to collect degrees if that is your thing, but if you lose sight of how real positive change is made in the workplace, you have lost before you began.

Like most things, it begins with relentlessly respecting others.

WHAT IT MEANS TO RELENTLESSLY RESPECT OTHERS

To ensure that this movement is built on a rock-solid foundation, we are going to need a clear and easily understood definition of the word *respect*. Unfortunately, we won't find it in a dictionary. Here is the official definition of *respect*, courtesy of Dictionary.com:

> ***Esteem for or a sense of the worth or excellence of a person, a personal quality or ability, or something considered as a manifestation of a personal quality or ability.***

Huh?

Now here's a shiny new definition of how we'll be looking at the word *respect*:

The consistent act of showing that you value a person's thoughts, ideas, feelings, and well-being.

This is the starting point for everything meaningful and worthwhile in the workplace. It is how we are able to bring out the best in others. Whether it is how we communicate with our team members, if we choose to clean up after ourselves at work, or if we fall into the trap of becoming a workplace bully, every one of our behaviors sends a clear message to others about our respect level for them.

There cannot be a movement to positively change anything in the workplace if we stumble at this first step. When we value people's thoughts, ideas, feelings, and well-being, it positively shapes our interactions with them in every possible way. Conversely, when we don't value those things in other people, it destroys the morale, civility, and effectiveness of any workplace on earth.

Here are three key truths when it comes to relentless respect in the workplace:

1. **Relentless respect is not affected by surface-level judgments.** Have you ever worked with a person who shows her customers the utmost respect, but is seemingly incapable of showing the same respect to her coworkers? Or maybe it is the manager who treats his boss and the other senior executives like royalty, but he treats his staff like second-class citizens? Or perhaps it's the person who treats the janitorial staff as if they were invisible, but would never dream of doing the same with the CEO? If so, you have seen the most common examples of conditional respect. The person whose behavior and respect level changes based solely on another person's job title, level of education, years of experience, or any other surface-level judgment is actively making the workplace (actually, the world) a less pleasant place for us all to live in.

2. **Relentless respect is not earned.** I used to work with a senior executive who literally would not speak to anyone who did not hold at least a manager job title. His rationale? They hadn't earned the right to speak to him yet. What he fails

to realize—and many other people like him—is that respect is not a competition. Relentless respect isn't something that someone needs to earn by jumping through hoops; it should be given freely and unconditionally to everyone. Of course, it is up to everyone to keep it. If you overheard a coworker making racist comments about a customer or you saw that your boss was having an extramarital affair with his administrative assistant, chances are you would lose respect for them. If you learned that one of your direct reports was a single mother who was working her way through college, all while being a shining example of workplace excellence, chances are that you would gain additional respect for her. Respect for someone can change over time, but the key is that everyone you meet should start from a place of relentless respect without the need to earn it first.

3. **Relentless respect cannot be gained through intimidation.** Sadly, there are many people in the workplace who regularly practice intimidation, fear, emotional outbursts, and bullying in hopes of gaining the respect of others. That might work in the short term to gain the compliance of others, but relentless respect will always elude people who do this expecting meaningful results in return. It is impossible to be relentlessly respected by others unless you are willing to consistently extend that same respect to them. Getting other people to comply is not an impressive achievement—anyone with the title of supervisor or above can make that happen with relative ease. But do you have what it takes to be relentlessly respected, not because of your job title or college degrees but because of who you are as a person? That is what this movement is all about.

The dusty old ideas that respect is based on surface-level judgments, needs to be earned, and is best gained through fear are dead. As Solutionists, our focus must be on consistently bringing out the best in others by relentlessly showing respect to them. If we want to use this edge to our advantage, we are going to have to engage in some tough training.

THE TRAINING GROUND: WHAT GETS INSPECTED GETS RESPECTED

We do not rise to the level of our expectations,
we fall to the level of our training.

—ARCHILOCHUS

This is a military quote from 650 BCE, and it has withstood the test of time because of its brilliance, truth, and universal application.

Before soldiers join the military, some of them have admitted to daydreaming about the excitement of hitting the battlefield for the first time. Their expectation is that they will morph into camouflaged badasses who will mow down the enemy forces like pixelated tough guys in a video game. Except something very different happens when they are on the battlefield for the first time. When the bullets are flying for real and there is no RESET button nearby to start over when they get shot, their expectations quickly become meaningless, because expectations don't save lives. Only one thing will—their training.

The goal of military training is to prepare soldiers for the harsh reality of war. Repeatedly executing maneuvers in full gear, in triple-digit heat. Repeatedly practicing reloading their weapons under severe duress. Repeatedly navigating near-exact replicas of buildings in environments that they will see in a firefight. All these exercises are designed to train the mind to do what's necessary when things get tough: Default to the training that will save your life, not to your expectations.

In the workplace, this is equally as valid. When things get tough, your energy is low, and your emotions are high, you might believe that you will respond respectfully, but when the pressure is on, your expectations will betray you. You will always react in the way that you are the most comfortable responding, which is the way you know best. And, just like on the battlefield, this can be either extremely useful or disastrous, depending on the quality of your training.

The fastest and most effective way to become expertly trained is to first become crystal clear about what it means to be relentlessly respectful at work. Then constantly repeat and practice those behaviors until they become our new normal.

Clearly, this is needed. Nearly 80 percent of Americans say that a lack of respect and courtesy is a serious national problem, and well over half of them (60 percent) say that it is only getting worse.[1]

Would you agree? If so, then it's time to stop relying on our expectations and common sense to save us. We need training.

Welcome to Respect Training 101. We've been expecting you.

THE THREE PILLARS OF RELENTLESS RESPECT

Using as our touchstone that we value a person's thoughts, ideas, feelings, and well-being, there are three pillars of relentless respect in the workplace that we must practice: (1) respectful communication, (2) respect for the individual, and (3) respect for the team.

Here are some responses that I received in all three areas from my workshop participants and blog readers from all over the world when they were asked, "What does it mean to be respectful in the workplace?":

1. Respectful Communication

- Communicating verbally and nonverbally in a manner that shows openness, not defensiveness.
- Consistently using common courtesy in all interactions, whether I have authority over the other person or not. For example, saying "Please" when I ask for something and "Thank you" after I receive it. Also, rejecting any excuse that I may have (for example, being too busy) *not* to do these things.
- Understanding that yelling, name-calling, and any other emotional outburst in anger has no place in a professional conversation. And if I happen to fall into that trap, I must quickly recognize it, own it, apologize for it, and do everything in my power to ensure that it does not happen again.
- Being aware that *how* we deliver the message—that is, our body language, our tone of voice, eye contact, and the like—is often more important than what we say.

- Using email appropriately and beginning each email with a proper salutation.
- Actively listening, being fully present, and not interrupting during conversations with others.
- Kindly greeting people when I see them and not purposefully ignoring them.

2. Respect for the Individual

- Never giving critical feedback in front of others.
- Being quick to apologize, own my mistakes, and offer solutions to make them right.
- Showing all the people in the organization a high level of respect, regardless of their job title or role.
- Quickly providing sincere praise, compliments, and gratitude to others for a job well done.
- Listening fully to others and consciously making an effort to make everyone I encounter feel important.

3. Respect for the Team

- Offering support to team members who need my help, without being asked.
- Respecting my team members' time and effort by showing up to work and to meetings on time, ready to work.
- Rejecting the temptation to create cliques at work or do anything to divide the team, instead of bringing it together.
- Actively being part of making my workplace a more positive place to work.

These are examples of relentless respect commitments, and they are just a start. A key aspect of this movement is to create your own statements of what it means to make your workplace, and life, work.

In case you were wondering, I'm fully committed to this, too. Here are my three relentless respect commitments, which I wrote down and practiced each day when I started on my journey to become part of the workplace solution. They still guide me to this day.

1. *Respectful communication:* When in conflict with someone else, I will have the courage to speak *to* the person, not *about* the person.

2. *Respect for the individual:* I will take full ownership for how my attitude, behavior, and words affect others.

3. *Respect for the team:* I will not leave work for others to do (whether it's picking up trash or actively changing the world) that I am more than capable of doing myself.

Just the act of keeping these three respect pillars in the forefront of my mind had a transformative effect on me and others. Like anything in life, the more I practiced these techniques, the more my skills in these areas grew and improved. After just a few weeks of daily reflection on these areas and actively demonstrating them, I had a new default set point. I literally trained myself to think and act differently.

The key is consistent and deliberate practice. Not when you feel like it. Not just with people you like. Not just once in a while. I'm talking about *relentlessly practicing this.* It is the only way to get better at things that are hard to do.

Okay, let's stop here for a moment. Do you feel it?

It is the urge to call this common sense.

Tempting, I know, but don't fall into that trap. Common sense is irrelevant, remember? We're talking about common practice here, and training and practice will help us get there in the shortest amount of time. The following objections to respect training have the exact opposite effect:

"I already know this stuff."

"I'm a grown man/woman, so don't insult my intelligence."

"I have more important things to deal with."

And my all-time favorite:

"Stop wasting my time. I have real work to do."

Isn't it ironic that the people who say these things are almost always the people who need respect training the most? Useless thoughts, like the ones above, have kept us trapped in disrespectful, unproductive, and unhealthy workplaces for far too long.

No one gives a damn about what you know; we only care about what you do. Nothing will improve in the workplace until we finally move past *thinking* we are doing the right thing, and start doing the right thing.

We are now at a crossroads. Are you going to take the action necessary to be part of the solution that your workplace desperately needs, or will you choose to be part of the problem that we are trying to fix?

MAKING A DIFFERENCE: BEING THE MOSQUITO

If you are ready to consistently practice the art of relentless respect, you might have the same self-defeating thought that I had when I started:

I'm too small to make a difference.

If you are currently dealing with a workplace environment where rudeness, incivility, gossip, and self-preservation at all costs rule the day, it is easy to think that simply being relentlessly respectful could never make any difference.

That thought is wrong.

My dad, who was born in Sierra Leone and is a retired University of Massachusetts professor, instilled this wisdom in me at a young age.

Once, after having a horrible day at school and lamenting that I was too small to make a difference, my dad lovingly pulled me aside and told me, "Whenever you think that you are too small to make a difference, try to fall asleep with a mosquito in the room."

He was right. Think about it. When a mosquito is buzzing by your ear as you try to go to sleep, even though it is tiny, it can have an enormous effect.

I think of this often when it comes to creating a more respectful workplace. All meaningful, widespread change starts at the individual level. It begins with one person deciding to make a difference.

One person who is willing to be the mosquito. You can do this if you choose to do it.

It's quite possible that you're reading these words and thinking,

> *I'm just a person on the front lines trying to survive each day in a toxic workplace. I'm not a supervisor, and people would laugh in my face if I ever suggested these ideas to them. Believe me, I work with some the meanest people imaginable who actively do the opposite of what you just described as relentless respect. I'm completely stuck.*

I absolutely hear you, but I'm here to say that you are not stuck. Even though you don't have a title, you are a leader. No matter who you are, where you work, and what you're dealing with, at the very least you can commit to the most important rule of leadership. It's actually the only rule of leadership that matters: leading by example.

This matters because relentless respect in the workplace isn't a cute fad or a fun experiment—we're starting a movement here. And this idea can only become a movement once a single person believes in an idea enough that he or she becomes committed to it. I believe that person is you.

Are you experiencing a lack of respect at work right now? If so, contributing to the problem by being disrespectful to those people in return won't solve anything. The key is to be willing to be the light that shines the way out of the darkness in your workplace or, as Mahatma Gandhi famously said, "Be the change that you want to see in the world."

Don't become the person who says, "What's the point in showering? I'm only going to get dirty again." Yes, of course you are going to get dirty again, but is that a good enough reason to give up showering forever? The same logic applies to relentless respect.

If no one else in your workplace is willing to do it, that means that it's up to you to answer the call each day. If not you, then who? You won't have to do this alone, but someone needs to get on the dance floor first.

For now, let's not worry about changing anyone else—this has to start with you. And that means that you may have to start this relentless respect journey while potentially dealing with the most disrespectful boss and colleagues imaginable. Here's something to keep in mind on this journey: The most useless workplace skill in the world is only being able to work effectively with people who are nice to you. That is not a skill that is capable of advancing you in your career. But being able to stay true to your values in the face of outward negativity? Now *that* is something that will advance you in your career and in your life.

Bringing out the best in others is the key to positively changing the world, and no college degrees or professional certifications can do that for you. Your willingness to embrace the interpersonal side of your job will allow you to be the change you want to see in the world.

You can't believe in the lie once you know the truth. Relentless respect is not common sense. Rather, this is how we will begin to finally make the workplace work again.

R.E.A.L. WORK

Assignment #1:

Welcome to the first of your twelve R.E.A.L. work assignments! This book is not designed to share some ideas and then hope that these ideas will somehow positively change the world. *They won't.* Changing the world is up to you and me—and it will require our action. That's why the next twelve chapters will each conclude with exercises to move us toward meaningful action.

Fair warning, the R.E.A.L. work assignments will be very challenging, even though they may appear easy. Even so, my challenge to you is simple: *Do the work.* The movement depends on it.

Create Your Relentless Respect Commitments

To ensure that you default to your training and not to your expectations, the first R.E.A.L. work assignment is to create three relentless respect commitments that will guide you in your interactions with others. Begin by writing down your answers to these three questions:

1. How will you communicate in a relentlessly respectful manner with others?
2. How will you show that you relentlessly respect each individual you encounter?
3. What action(s) will you take to show that you relentlessly respect the team?

Once you have come up with those statements, each day deliberately practice putting these statements into action. Do not become one of the many people who let their moods determine their manners. You're not off the hook when you're feeling under the weather, faced with a stressful deadline, or when you are dealing with a challenging colleague. I'm using the word *relentless* for a reason.

Most of all, don't let anyone else stop you from keeping these commitments. Neither your unbearable coworker nor your micromanaging boss deserves that kind of power over you. Instead, take ownership of your relentless respect commitments to become the person who will actively create a more respectful work environment.

CHAPTER

5

CONNECTING TO YOUR "HIRE" SELF

Choosing Self-Accountability

It is easy to dodge our responsibilities, but we cannot dodge the consequences of dodging our responsibilities.

—JOSIAH STAMP

You might not be aware of this, but you have an unpaid debt that you need to pay someone.

It has been a while, so you might not recognize the person you are indebted to, but there is no doubt that you know this person *very* well. We are going to get reacquainted with this person but, first, let's imagine a very common workplace scenario.

I want you to picture a person interviewing for a dream job.

Chances are that the interviewee was full of hope, promise, and excitement prior to the interview. Most likely, this eager job candidate researched the company website with the single-minded dedication of a detective searching for clues in a high-profile murder case. This person was ready to shine brightly, and coolly answer any question that the interviewer asked. For example:

"Tell me about a time when you had to deal with a difficult customer or colleague. What techniques did you use to come to an amicable resolution?"

I'm sure that this candidate smiled, looked the interviewer confidently in the eye, and said, "I'm very skilled in dealing with difficult personalities. There was a time when I had to work with someone who was fairly rude, but I was able to deal with her by focusing on her positive traits, staying calm, and always stressing the common goal that we shared—which, in this case, was taking care of our customers. In the end, we were able to work together quite well and we built a solid working relationship because I always showed her respect. I'm confident that I could use the same skills in any difficult professional situation that I will encounter."

Nice answer. Do you know who said those words?

You did.

More specifically, it was your *"Hire Self"* aka the person you said you were in order to get hired for your current job.

I doubt that when the interviewer asked you that question you responded, "When someone gives me an attitude, I'm quick to put a finger in his face and start acting ignorant. Nobody disrespects me unless he's planning on making an emergency trip to see his dentist. Believe me."

No sane person would ever say that in an interview. So how come employees in workplaces all over the world routinely go down the aforementioned dead-end road when they are faced with a difficult colleague, customer, or boss? Are they all a bunch of shady, pathological liars, who would say or do anything to get hired?

No, I don't believe that our Hire Selves were performing award-winning acting jobs or telling flat-out lies.

Our Hire Self is the ideal we believed we could achieve when dealing with challenging situations, difficult people, and workplace negativity—that's why we said what we said. But once the interview ends and the real work begins, it is easy to forget that.

The thing is we can't forget that. It was our Hire Self who got us the job, our Hire Self is allowing us to keep the lights on in our homes and feed our kids, and most importantly, our Hire Self is the person who represents the absolute best version of our self. We owe quite a bit to this person, and there is only one way to pay this debt.

Full accountability.

Full accountability is the steadfast willingness to fully own the outcomes of our words, actions, and behavior—and it is the core of Hire Selves all over the world. Would you want to hire a babysitter who is only partially willing to take responsibility for watching and caring for your one-year-old child? Would you want to fly on a plane with a pilot who is not willing to fully own her responsibility to land the plane safely? Would you be willing to be operated on by a surgical team who is unwilling to take ownership for the success of your surgery? Would you hire someone who avoids taking ownership consistently?

If so, you are far braver than I am.

Our Hire Self said that we would pass on the tempting indulgences of casting blame and making excuses, and that we would own our actions—all of them—instead. And that is exactly what we need to do to positively change our workplaces: Own it. It starts with us keeping our promise to the highest part of our self.

This is the heart of self-accountability.

THE FRENCH FRY APOCALYPSE: A STORY OF ACCOUNTABILITY

Accountability. Never before has one simple word held so much power to build, or completely destroy, any professional environment on earth.

Without accountability there is little hope of creating any meaningful positive change in our workplaces, our personal lives, or any place in between. But before you run out to hold everyone else accountable, I want you to do something that is much more important and meaningful.

Hold yourself accountable.

Here's one of the best examples of self-accountability that I have ever seen.

When I was in college, my buddies and I decided to hit up the local twenty-four-hour fast food restaurant after a long night of partying, in hopes of stuffing our faces with greasy food before we went to bed. Although this was a regular Saturday night occurrence, something was about to happen that would make this night stand out in my mind forever.

As we approached the counter to place our order, our worst nightmare came true: Inexplicably, the restaurant had somehow run out of French fries.

Yes, this was definitely far from a big deal, but to four well-partied and ravenously hungry college guys, it was similar to telling a room full of kindergartners that Santa Claus, the Tooth Fairy, and the Easter Bunny had all died in a fiery plane crash. It was not a pleasant scene.

But here is where it gets interesting.

There were only three employees in the restaurant that night: the cashier, the fry cook, and the night manager. All three of these people took turns dealing with this issue in completely different ways.

The cashier just threw up her hands and said, "Hey, it's not my fault. I'm just working the cash register. I don't cook the food."

After hearing all the commotion out front, the fry cook poked his head out from the back and sarcastically said, "Give us a break. There's no magical French fry fairy who's going to make French fries appear out of thin air. If she existed, we would have called her already. There's nothing we can do. Just order something else."

The crowd was getting more and more irritated. Then the night manager appeared and directly addressed everyone who was waiting to order—at that point, there were ten to twelve angry people in front of the register. What she said next was simple, powerful, and has stayed with me for close to twenty years.

"I am so sorry for the French fry shortage. As the manager, I own this one. The shipment won't be here until nine a.m. In the meantime, please don't take your frustrations out on my employees. If you are upset about this, please address your anger at me."

Whoa. Now *that's* accountability.

She didn't blame the French fry suppliers. She didn't hide in the back like a coward and allow her employees to take the heat. This woman stood up like the boss she was by fully owning the fact that there were no French fries, and she squarely put herself in the line of fire against a crowd of boozed-up, annoyed, and hungry college kids. The result was a few grumbles, but, overwhelmingly, the customers—myself included—gained a deep level of respect for her courage and applauded her for it. I'm sure her employees loved her for it, too.

There is a big problem with this story, though. Did you catch it?

Why didn't the cashier and fry cook take accountability?

Surely, the cashier and the fry cook knew that they were temporarily out of French fries. But instead, they did nothing. Unless you are mistaking the act of helplessly throwing their arms in the air and making lame jokes about French fry fairies for "doing something."

There is magic in what the manager did. And for this movement to become real, we need to tap into what made her fearlessly stare down a hungry mob in the middle of the night.

WHAT DO YOU OWN?

That manager took complete ownership of that situation. If you are thinking, *Well, that's what the manager is supposed to do. She's the boss . . .* , you are missing the point. Any one of the three of those employees could have done the exact same thing she did, but they didn't.

Since you weren't there with me at that fast food restaurant many years ago, you didn't get to see the power of that response firsthand. So let's bring it back to present day and consider this potentially career-altering and life-changing question:

Do you have what it takes to do what the manager did that night? And, if so, would you be willing to do what she did consistently?

What she did was take full ownership—that's what your Hire Self would do, and it's what I'm asking you to do as a Solutionist.

The movement depends on it.

Before you say that you're all in, let's be clear on what taking ownership means. In the spirit of full disclosure, there is nothing fun or easy about any of this—that's why so many people are unwilling or unable to do it. If you are ready to do it anyway, this is what it requires. In every situation in your professional life, you will ask yourself the most empowering accountability question in the world:

What part of this situation do I own?

This question is empowering because the answer puts you in control. And what you control, you can change.

That coworker whose questionable morals prompt her to steal the credit for your hard work? You now own part of that. Your boss who is overloading you with work and riding you like American Pharaoh for forty-plus hours a week? You own a piece of that, too. The annoying client who has a habit of calling you after 10:00 p.m. every night to ask you questions that could easily wait until the morning? You guessed it—part of that is on you, my friend.

I'm not saying that any of those things are your fault, mind you. You can't control how other people are acting, so you can't own that. This is about us relentlessly owning every ounce of what is within our power to own and refusing to cede any of that power to another person. Least of all to someone who does not deserve it.

So what are the things we own and will always completely belong to us?

Our decisions belong to us. Our actions, effort, and willingness to show up fully belong to us. Our daily attitudes belong to us. Most of all, our response to anything or anyone that is keeping us from creating a more positive workplace belongs to us. No one has the power to affect any of this unless we give them the power to do so—and giving away this power is the most self-destructive mistake we can make.

If your boss is making your life a living hell and you feel helpless to do anything about it, you have already lost before you began. Dwelling on how poorly she treats you and how she's eroding your mental health on a daily basis will accomplish nothing, except to weaken your resolve and strengthen your sense of victimhood. Neither of which will change the reality that your boss is still a raging jerk, and that you haven't done anything to solve that problem. Remember this—you are only helpless if you are unconscious or dead.

The life-limiting choice to remain a victim is a choice to remain powerless, and you are not a victim. Just the simple act of asking yourself, *What part of this do I own?* can change everything because it shifts your focus to your own source of power.

- You can own that you are often baited by your boss's passive-aggressiveness and choose to rise above that in the future.
- You can own that you have allowed your boss to cross the line by saying wildly inappropriate things to you, and choose to step up and do something about it (if you don't know how to do this, chapters 10 and 11 will help).
- You can own that you alone are responsible for your happiness, mental health, and professional success—not your boss or anyone else.
- You can own the process of plotting your exit strategy by looking hard for another job.

Choosing ownership means that you are no longer allowing the situation to control you. The restaurant manager was only able to take control, calm the mob, and create a positive situation for herself and others once she stepped up and owned the situation.

Are you ready to take ownership?

If so, we need to do a little killing first.

KILLING THE TWINS: BLAME AND EXCUSES

There is a cost to this kind of thinking. It means that we fully have to reject the following ways of thinking:

There's nothing I can do. It's hopeless.

Hey, I did my part.

I would have been able to do it, if it weren't for [insert excuse here].

It's his or her fault, not mine.

To truly honor our Hire Selves and accept the responsibility of making our workplaces work, we will need to swiftly kill the twins of workplace mediocrity: blame and excuses.

This might be tough to hear, but if you have a burning need to be right at all costs, this movement is not for you.

Blame and excuses are the first line of defense for a person who is not ready, and this kind of person is fundamentally incapable of positively changing any workplace. Do you think you would ever be hired for a job if you routinely shared in job interviews that you blame everyone else for your shortcomings, you happily stab your colleagues in the back the moment things go south, and that you are always right? Doubtful.

We are climbing a steep mountain here, and our journey will become much tougher, if not impossible, if we are carrying these two unruly twins on our backs the entire time.

So, before you take the first step, ask yourself this when you face your next workplace challenge: Is it more appealing to assign blame or to solve the problem? Solutionists solve. That's what we do. Leave the blame and excuses for the other people who are driven by the ego-fueled need to be right. We need to be driven by something more meaningful: the need to solve the problem.

A customer just tripped over a toy in the middle of the aisle of your store, and he appeared to severely injure his leg. A patient just acquired an infection from a piece of medical equipment that was not properly sterilized. The food that you just served to the patrons in the VIP section of your restaurant had a long, scraggly hair in it.

At this point, does it really matter who is right or wrong? Do your excuses and blame really matter to the people who are negatively affected? They won't change the facts, that's for sure. The facts are that you have a problem on your hands, and it needs to be solved. Quickly.

If others want to spin their wheels by slinging blame around, even if some of that undeserved blame is directed at you, let them. Just don't waste any of your time joining in on their foolishness. While they are crying over spilled milk, be the one grabbing the paper towels.

What the blame-slingers and excuse-makers are missing is that they are dead weight that is slowing down our ascent to the goal just by their presence. Being a world-class blame-slinger or excuse-maker is not something you want on your resume. Solving problems is what people want to see. The only people capable of positively dealing with the problems of our world are the ones who are willing to own their part in solving them.

In other words, you must cultivate the habit of being quick to own and slow to blame.

THIS IS NOT ABOUT ANYONE ELSE

Now it's time for the hard part.

I want you to think of the most irritating and difficult coworker you currently work with. In other words, think of the person you believe needs to hear this message the most. Got that person in your mind? Good.

That person doesn't come anywhere close to needing this message as much as you do.

Ouch. Don't take it personally.

If you think we can change the workplace by waiting for the most challenging, difficult, and obstinate coworkers to magically wake up and see the warm glowing light of workplace positivity, you are sadly mistaken. This is our journey, not theirs.

I have seen countless people in my classes and seminars who pitifully give their power away to these people by defiantly declaring, "I'll change when he changes! That's when I'll change!"

Here's something troubling to think about: What if he doesn't change?

I have burned too many years off my time line waiting for the negative influences in our workplaces to wake up and finally get it. Breathlessly, I hoped that someone else would step up to make the workplace a more positive place for me and others, and, not surprisingly, my hero hasn't arrived yet.

I'm done.

From now on I'm going to be my own hero. No more waiting for someone to arrive at the front door with a bouquet of flowers. We're empowered to pick our own damn flowers.

This empowerment is a gift that should not be squandered. Positively changing our workplaces does not require anyone else to do the right thing. It only requires *you* to do the right thing. This movement will reach critical mass only if you commit to taking full ownership of your part in this process. Don't worry about what everyone else is doing. If you are awake, the key is to stay awake—regardless of how many people around you are asleep.

Taking ownership and full accountability for being a positive influence is the only way we can save ourselves and others. It's also the only way to live the highest version of ourselves.

After all, that is what your Hire Self would do.

R.E.A.L. WORK

Assignment #2:

Owning Adversity

For this assignment, I want you to write down at least three things that are happening in your current job that are less than ideal.

Once you have written them down, I want you to ask yourself, "What part of these situations do I own?" Saying "None" is not an answer that will serve you. Face reality. What choices did you make or fail to make? Is there something you could have done differently? Challenge yourself.

By entertaining the notion that you own a piece of everything that is happening to you at work, you get to keep your power instead of giving it away to blaming or excuse-making. Admittedly, this is a challenging exercise, but it is by far one of the most rewarding. Shifting our perspective about how we view the challenges in our path gives us the power to determine how much we will allow those challenges to affect us.

CHAPTER

6

NUMBER ONE

Relentlessly Respecting Ourselves

Creating healthy boundaries is not an act of defiance, but a prerequisite for self-preservation. Don't let anyone tell you otherwise.

—TOMIKO FRASER

This might be the most important chapter in this book.

We will encounter many roadblocks as we make this workplace positivity movement a reality, but none that will stop us in our well-intentioned tracks faster than failing to relentlessly respect ourselves. Let's start with a brief cautionary tale.

Allow me to introduce you to Brian.

Brian was one of those guys who prided himself on putting in twelve- to thirteen-hour days at the office and for giving anyone a vicious side eye if they packed up to leave the office after only putting in a pedestrian eight hours. Admittedly, just that look alone kept me at my cubicle well past quitting time more often than I'd like to admit.

Besides putting in long hours and shaming others for not doing the same, there was something else that Brian was known for around the office. He would loudly brag to anyone who would listen that he had not taken *any* vacation days in over five years. Even though I was at the beginning of my professional life when I worked with him, I never understood why he viewed vacations as a life staple of the undedicated and lazy. Perhaps he thought that hard workers don't take vacations. Who knows?

What I did know was that every day I worked with him he looked like he was on the brink of death.

Can you guess how Brian's story turned out?

No, he didn't collapse and die on the job, thankfully. But he did end up with heart trouble, his marriage broke up, and his two children barely even knew who he was. In the cruelest twist of all, due in large part to his practice of overworking himself past the point of exhaustion, the quality of his work deteriorated so much that he was eventually let go by the company.

You read that right. After giving many devoted years to his company, the rewards for his dedication were a stress-induced heart condition, a divorce, and a pitifully small severance package that probably kept him financially afloat for a month. That doesn't sound like a fair trade-off to me.

I will never know what Brian's motivation was in thoroughly burning himself out in that manner. He didn't seem joyful, healthy, or particularly good at his job while I worked with him. Ironically, it might have been possible for him to have been all three of those things if he took the time to pump the brakes and take care of himself.

So what does this all mean?

Is Brian just an extreme example of a misguided, self-loathing masochist who doesn't know when to stop? There is a danger in believing that. Upon deeper inspection, his story is a common one, and it's not as extreme as you may think. It may even be the story that you are currently writing for yourself right now.

If so, this chapter is written in hopes of helping you craft a different story.

Don't get me wrong—if you deeply love your job and you find your bliss in working sixty-plus hours a week, then by all means, keep doing what you are doing. But, chances are, if that were the case, you wouldn't be reading this book in the first place.

On the other hand, if you are one of the millions of people whose health, happiness, and overall quality of life are being negatively affected by overworking yourself, then it's time for you to take a stand to reclaim your life before it's too late. I am happy to stand with you.

Contrary to popular American belief these days, more is not always more—especially when it comes to the hours you are putting in at the workplace.

The moral of Brian's story, and the similar stories of many other people I have worked with, is a powerful one that came through loud and clear:

In order to have a positive experience at work, we need to relentlessly respect ourselves, too.

The consequences of failing to do this could be catastrophic.

LIVING TO WORK IS WORKING TO DIE

Just to be clear, I have nothing against hard work.

I do have something against engaging in activities that will put us in the grave far sooner than necessary. And there is little doubt that repeated sixty-plus-hour workweeks without taking a meaningful break will do that. Can our bodies endure going all-out for short bursts or for certain seasons? Sure. Can we sustain this pace indefinitely? Not without significant damage in the long run.

My problem is with overworking, and it has reached full-blown-crisis status in America. The statistics that support this are both fascinating and horrifying.

- In a study of twenty-one countries (sixteen European countries, plus Australia, Canada, Japan, New Zealand, and the United States), the United States is the only one that does not require employers to provide paid vacation time to their employees. In case you are wondering, that is an unfortunate similarity that we share with the likes of North Korea.[1]

- According to the International Labour Organization, Americans work 137 more hours per year than Japanese workers (yes, the same Japanese culture that created the term *karoshi*, which means "death by overwork"),

260 more hours per year than British workers, and 499 more hours per year than French workers.[2]

- The average American only takes half of his or her allotted vacation time.[3]
- Of those who do take a break from the grind, a disturbingly high 61 percent admitted to doing some work while on vacation.[4]
- And, least surprising of all, one in three Americans are chronically overworked.[5]

As bad as these statistics are, they do not even touch on the life-diminishing effects that the stress of overwork can have on our health and well-being. Skipping meals, overloading our nervous system with caffeinated drinks, and being sleep-deprived are bad enough. Sadly, those are usually the gateway to more serious problems that the stress of overwork can create, such as heightened anxiety, increased risk for heart attack or stroke, depression, type 2 diabetes, and a descent into dangerous addictions, such as alcoholism and drug abuse.

Do you know what makes all of this even more tragic? The fact that overworking does not increase our productivity and effectiveness in any way. Studies show that overworking decreases both, while increasing our potential for mistakes significantly.

This should not be surprising. Picture an endurance athlete who is asked to perform at a high level for months and months without any meaningful rest periods to recharge. Predictably, she will eventually lose focus, become less effective in competitions, physically and mentally break down, and likely wind up in a hospital. Why would working at *anything* nonstop be any different?

Humans are not built to expend a significant amount of energy indefinitely. If we fail to take the time to meaningfully rejuvenate and refresh our brains and bodies on a regular basis, at best we will devolve into below-average employees, and at worst, we are accelerating our own death.

This is the height of insanity.

If we know that overworking ourselves and choosing not to take vacations will lead to decreased productivity, increased mistakes on the job, greater risk for physical and mental health issues, and an inevitable descent into misery and unhappiness for ourselves and those we love, why do we do this to ourselves?

I know why.

More importantly, I know what we need to do about it.

RETHINKING OUR PRIORITIES

More than ever, people are tethered to their smartphones, tablets, and laptops during off-hours. Some say our obsession with instant communication keeps us chained to our devices, even when we are outside the office. I think it's something darker than that.

It is fear that keeps us attached.

The fears are almost too numerous to count. We fear not looking like a team player if we are not responsive to our colleagues' needs. We fear falling behind in our work if we don't spend our free time away from the office working. We fear missing out on something critical. We fear looking like slackers in comparison to our more responsive colleagues. We fear being punished for not being available. We fear getting fired.

For some reason, those fears take precedence over what should truly scare us: *the fear of looking back on our lives only to realize that we had it wrong the whole time.*

We fear our colleagues passive-aggressively rolling their eyes at us if we leave the office on time but not the impact that our repeated absence at the dinner table will have on our young children. We fear our boss's wrath if we don't commit to sustaining the unsustainable, but we don't fear the steep price this commitment will inflict on our health. We fear being irrelevant or replaced at the office, but we don't fear the irrelevance of being alone, burned out, or dead.

Our priorities are out of order and, in some cases, they are nonexistent. Until we address this, overwork—or, worse, *other people's priorities*—will be our masters.

So, what are your priorities? In other words, in comparison to everything going on in your work life, what are the key activities that really deserve most of your attention, energy, and time?

Is it increasing the amount of quality time with your children?

Is it reclaiming your health? Is it enjoying the fun and happiness of being around your buddies? Is it reconnecting spiritually? Is it rekindling the spark with your significant other? Only you can answer these questions, and you must. This will be a big part of the R.E.A.L. work at the end of this chapter.

Until we get there, just know this—since you cannot do it all—your priorities here are to focus your attention, your energy, and your time on what truly matters. Unfortunately, if you are not crystal clear on your priorities, you have officially given anyone else in your life the power to control your priorities for you, by default. This is how very smart people are persuaded to do some very dumb things, like working sixty hours a week for months on end until they collapse.

This is far too important an issue to be ignored. Decide what really matters in your life and choose to live deliberately, instead of by chance.

It's not up to your employer, your boss, or anyone else in your life to make your well-being and your best life a priority. It's your health and it's your life, so it is your responsibility to relentlessly respect yourself.

This cannot be done without drawing some very clear lines.

THE NEW WORK-LIFE BALANCE: WORK-LIFE SEPARATION

I have always hated the term *work-life balance.*

The term is fundamentally flawed because *balance* implies that there will be a point at which both our work lives and our personal lives will be evenly distributed. According to the Bureau of Labor Statistics, this is mathematically impossible. On average we spend 8.9 hours of our 24-hour day working or doing work-related activities and 7.7 hours a day asleep,[6] which means that we have already committed the majority of our waking hours to our job. Chasing the elusive ghost of work-life balance is not a pursuit that is worthy of your effort.

More modern ideas like work-life integration are not any better at fixing our overwork problems. How is the idea of mixing our work lives and our personal lives together, until we cannot discern one from the other, a helpful pursuit? It's this kind of antilogic that makes some of you take conference calls while you're on your honeymoon or respond to an endless sea of emails while your son is tugging on your leg to play. Consistently bringing your work duties into your personal life will eventually create more problems than it solves.

My goal for this movement is work-life separation.

Instead of viewing your life as one big pie chart, where you are hopelessly attempting to balance your professional work and personal life, what if you viewed your professional work and your personal life as *two separate pie charts*? This simple shift in perspective changes everything, because instead of fighting the losing battle of balancing your work duties with your personal life, you are now able to give 100 percent to both, without comparing the percentage of time given to either one.

The only fight you need to be concerned about is the fight to keep the work you do and your personal life as separate as possible. While you are enjoying your personal time at home with your family, on vacation, or having fun with your buddies on the weekend, you are not allowing your work duties to creep into that time. This is a fight that you can win but not without clear boundaries.

NECESSARY BOUNDARIES

If our priorities are how we would like to focus our attention, energy, and time, our boundaries are the limits we put in place to protect those priorities. And steadfast protection is crucial.

A life without boundaries is like living in a house with a permanently wide-open front door. Doing so would leave you and your loved ones at heightened risk for vandalism, theft, assault, and potentially, much worse. Of course, not everyone has questionable motives when they see your wide-open door, but you are kidding yourself if you think that no one does. The door is the first line of protection for your home, just as boundaries are the first line of defense for your priorities.

Let me give you a real-life example of my priorities and how I use clear boundaries to protect them from the demands of the workplace.

Here are my priorities (in no particular order):

- Being a fully present father to my two little girls (seven and four years old, as I'm writing this). This includes being there for every dance recital, soccer game, and any other important event in their lives.
- Sleeping at least six hours a night (preferably eight or nine, but no less than six).
- Actively taking care of my physical health through exercise and smart food choices.
- Staying in close contact with my parents and my friends.
- Spending quality time with my wife that does not include staring at any glowing blue boxes (television, laptop, cell phone, and the like).
- Frequent downtime to rest and recharge in order to be my best for my family, friends, and colleagues (watching sports, going on vacation, taking a nap, etc.).
- Engaging in lifelong learning (my personal favorites are reading, listening to podcasts, going to seminars, and watching TED talks) to maximize my effectiveness as a leader, a father, a husband, and a human being.
- Maintaining a deep spiritual connection through daily meditation and mindfulness practices.
- Being able to express my creativity through writing, public speaking, and my other hobbies.

These are the things that keep me grounded, peaceful, happy, and effective. When I allow work, or anything else, to get in the way of these priorities, I fall short of my potential as a human being. This unfortunate outcome is guaranteed when we give our power away and let someone else control how we use our attention, energy, and time.

That is not going to work for us. If we want to experience a fuller life, we cannot make a habit of showing up at any less than our absolute best.

Here are the boundaries I have in place to ensure that these priorities stay protected as much as possible:

- When I am out of the office on vacation, whether it's just for one day or two weeks, I do not answer work-related email or calls. *Ever.* I don't care who is trying to contact me. I devote practically three hundred days each year to my job—my vacation time is mine.
- Speaking of which, I proudly use as much of my vacation time as possible. I earned it, so I use it.
- I leave the office every night no later than 5:30 p.m. to ensure that I'm home for dinner with my wife and girls.
- Since I can be easily tempted, I leave all my work-related devices at home when I'm on an extended vacation. Sometimes, just the act of reading an email from certain people is enough to send my mood into an easily avoidable tailspin.
- I leave the office for lunch every day, and I don't eat lunch at my desk. It is a daily reminder for me to get off my arse, move my eyes away from the computer screen, and get some fresh air.

These simple boundaries are wildly effective in keeping my priorities from being affected by the needs of the workplace. Equally as important, these boundaries allow me to be a more wildly effective employee. When I'm at work, I am *on* and my employer consistently gets 100 percent of my best effort on a daily basis. The main reason this is possible is that while I am away from work, I am giving 100 percent of my time to my priorities, which, in turn, gives me the energy to give my all at work each day. I treat my time away from work as seriously as my time spent at work.

Instead of it being a vicious cycle, work-life separation is a cycle of self-love and self-respect.

I know what you're thinking.

You might have read my boundary list and thought, "That must be nice for him, but there's a better chance of me getting drafted by the Los Angeles Lakers than there is of me putting any of those crazy boundaries into place in my world."

If so, I wouldn't blame you. I spent most of my adult life believing that approach was insane, until I had no choice but to implement those boundaries. It took me a while, but eventually I became intimately acquainted with the most powerful two-letter word in the known universe.

And if a nonconfrontational, people-pleasing guy like myself can master it, I am convinced that anyone else can do it, too.

THE POSITIVE POWER OF NO

I am just going to come out and say it: You cannot experience any meaningful professional success or enjoy any personal peace without the ability to say no.

Having priorities is a critically important start, but other people have priorities, too—and sometimes they won't align with yours. Boundaries are also necessary, but without the courage to enforce them, you will end up stuck where you started.

No addresses both those pesky issues. The word *no* is what changes everything. It is where the rubber hits the road when it comes to relentlessly respecting ourselves in the workplace, or anywhere else for that matter.

Seven years ago, shortly after my first daughter was born, I had a workaholic boss who had an extremely annoying habit of approaching my cubicle ten minutes before I was about to leave and engaging me in conversation. Sometimes it was about sharing details from a meeting that she had attended earlier in the day. Sometimes it was to get an update from me that could wait until the following day. Sometimes she had to tell me a mind-numbing story about her pets.

Every time, I wanted to jam a pencil into my ear or call for the sweet angel of death to swoop in and save me from my misery.

Until one evening, everything changed.

As usual, she came by my cubicle at 4:50 p.m. to talk about her latest drama with her pets. Ten minutes of nodding and smiling at her stories turned into thirty minutes. Then, thirty minutes turned into an hour. My phone vibrated with concerned texts from my wife, "Where are you? Are you okay?" as I glanced helplessly at my phone and continued to feign interest in Fluffy's latest escapades. I felt like a hostage. Finally, seventy-five minutes after when I should have left, my boss finally said, "You really should leave now. You have a baby at home."

Gee, thanks.

My fury raged inside me as I sat in bumper-to-bumper traffic for an additional forty-five minutes—traffic that could have been avoided if I had left the office on time. When I finally arrived at home nearly two hours later, I still remember the look of raw anguish on my sleep-deprived wife's face as I opened the door to my apartment and weakly explained why I was late. She handed me my one-month-old daughter who was crying hysterically, and with tears also in her eyes, my wife said, "Why do you keep letting her do this to you? I need you here on time."

That moment was the start of everything for me. *Why was I letting her do this to me?* Why was I waiting for my boss to honor me and the time that I needed with my newborn baby? That was not my boss's responsibility. It was mine.

The next evening at 4:45 p.m., it happened again—my boss started up another nonessential conversation about a meeting that she had attended earlier in the day. This time, I was armed with my priorities in order, my boundary in place, and a new resolve to relentlessly respect myself. When the clock hit 5:00 p.m., I politely interrupted her story and said the following:

"I really need to go and be with my wife and baby. Let's pick this up tomorrow morning when I get back to the office. Have a great night and I'll see you first thing tomorrow."

She had a look of surprise on her face as I packed up my stuff and started walking toward the door. I could feel my heart practically beating in my throat, but I pushed through my fears and did not look back until I got safely into my car.

This might sound silly, but it was one of the most empowering moments of my life. I effectively enforced a boundary and relentlessly respected myself. I actually pumped my fist in the air as I drove out of the parking lot as if I had just won the heavyweight championship of the world.

You might not be comfortable walking out on your boss as I did that night, and I'm not saying that you should do anything like that. What I do want you to do is to get comfortable with consistently enforcing your boundaries, starting today.

Ready to draw the line in the sand?

Good. Here's how to do it.

DRAWING THE L.I.N.E.

Keep in mind that making the choice to honor your boundaries comes with no guarantees. Standing up for yourself and your priorities may not go well.

I could tell that my boss was annoyed that I did not embrace her workaholic, think-about-work-24/7 mentality. She passive-aggressively dumped extra work on me as my reward for walking out on her at my scheduled quitting time and for putting my family first, but it didn't matter. I was at the point at which I was ready to accept any consequence as a result of staying true to my boundaries. The alternative choice was to dishonor myself by staying late and missing out on special moments with my daughter. For what? To avoid temporarily upsetting my boss by leaving on time after putting in a full day's work? Not a chance.

I made the right choice. Seven years later, my former boss is long gone and my bond with my daughter and her little sister is stronger than ever. I often wonder if that would be the case if I had continually failed to honor my boundaries.

That is my question for you.

What is the alternative if you choose to go another day without honoring your boundaries? What do you stand to lose, personally and professionally, if you ignore your priorities? I'm dead serious about this. I want you to get clear on this because, depending on your situation, that clarity could be the spark that inspires you to act.

If you have decided to no longer let people violate your boundaries, you are ready to draw the line. Or, more specifically, the L.I.N.E.

L.I.N.E. is an acronym that stands for Listen, Inspect, NO, and

Enforce, and it is a useful tool for protecting your priorities and enforcing your boundaries. This is the process:

Listen: If someone is asking you to do something that may violate your boundaries, this is not the time to get defensive. Listen fully, do not interrupt, and check the emotions that may be bubbling up inside you. It's tempting, but don't skip this step. Saying no becomes much more difficult if you are interrupting, getting defensive, or showing in your face that you are already annoyed. Stay calm, check your emotions, and listen fully.

Inspect: Once you are clear about your boundaries, you need to determine if what is being asked of you violates one of those boundaries. Obviously, this step cannot be completed without knowing your boundaries, so if you haven't done that yet, you'll have a chance to at the end of this chapter. If your boundary has been violated, move onto the next step.

NO: Now it's time for some action. Say no, and be clear when you say it—leave no room for confusion. Saying, "I can't right now, but maybe I can sometime in the future," is *not* a no. All you are doing is kicking the can down the road and leaving your no for later. Do it now instead. Remember, this is not about saying no to the other person; this is solely about saying yes to yourself.

Enforce: If you found the courage to say no, then own that no. Waffling, being wishy-washy, or, worst of all, changing your no to a yes after you get challenged (especially when *no* is what you really wanted to say) will destroy your self-esteem and make you look like a joke. Enforce your no by honoring your boundaries.

Let's take a look at what this would look like in action:

Example #1:

Your work team needs your help and wants you to come into work on a Saturday.

Listen <stay calm and listen fully without interrupting>: "Hey Shola, a few of us from our work team are coming in this Saturday to help prepare for the big visit from the CEO and her executive team on

Monday. We could really use your help getting everything together. Are you in?"

Inspect <think to yourself>: Normally, I wouldn't have a problem coming into work for an occasional Saturday, but this Saturday is my daughter's soccer game and it is a priority for me to be there for her games. This is a boundary violation.

NO: "Sorry, I have a prior family engagement on Saturday and I can't make it."

Challenge: "Hey, we had other plans, too, and we're still going into the office. Be a team player, man."

Enforce: "These plans are unchangeable and I'm not going to make it in on Saturday. If you need any extra help on Monday morning before she arrives, I'll be available then."

Example #2:

Your boss is calling your cell phone at 8:00 p.m. on Friday night while you are enjoying a date night with your spouse. You sent the first call directly to voice mail, but he called back immediately afterward.

Listen <stay calm and listen fully without interrupting>: "Shola, I just got off the plane and I'm really curious to know how the budget meeting went this afternoon. I cannot wait to hear the details!"

Inspect <think to yourself>: This is a nonemergency issue that can wait until Monday. Also, my wife and I are only able to get one date night a month, if we're lucky. This is the rare and sacred time when we don't have to talk about our kids, our drama, and our jobs for a couple of hours. This phone call is a huge boundary violation.

NO: "The budget meeting went well. I'm having dinner with my wife right now, but I will be happy to fill you in on the details on Monday."

Challenge: "Give me a call when you're done with dinner."

Enforce: "I'm sorry, we're having a date night and we're planning on being out late. I'll give you the full details on Monday."

Time for a bit of self-disclosure: *This process scared the hell out of me the first few times I used it.* I thought it would be easier to say yes while suffering in silence, instead of saying no and potentially rocking the boat. I was wrong. Habitually saying yes when you mean no makes nothing easier. It only leaves you burned out, deeply resentful, and unable to bring your best self to work. There is nothing easy about that.

Yes, it is scary to stand up for your priorities when you have never done it before, but if you don't stand up for them, no one else will.

WHAT WE ALLOW IS WHAT WILL CONTINUE

As the third part of the foundation in this movement, I need this message to stick:

What we allow is what will continue.

If you don't find the courage to protect your priorities and boundaries, you are effectively allowing your priorities and boundaries to be controlled by other people. Yes, you are allowing it. We must think and act differently in order to experience a different outcome.

Do not let anyone fool you into thinking that you are lazy or selfish if you choose to enforce your boundaries. If you are reading this book, I am assuming that you have a bias toward hard work and for honoring your Hire Self. I want us to work hard. But instead of working hard at unimportant things, I want us to work hard at what matters. I believe in giving it our all while we're at work, but I'm calling for a separation.

Yes, you have to put food on the table and do whatever is necessary to keep the lights on in your home—believe me, I get it. But you cannot sustain a lifestyle of going nonstop until you drop. You cannot afford to choose work over your relationships only to realize that those relationships have decided to move on without you once you finally come to your senses.

We must give ourselves permission to walk away from the laptop or the company-issued cell phone and grab some crayons to playfully create doodle-filled masterpieces with our kids.

We must give ourselves permission to tell our colleagues and our bosses that, unless it's urgent, work inquiries should only be made during work hours.

We must give ourselves permission to take vacations in order to renew, recharge, and reconnect with our loved ones with depth and meaning.

We must give ourselves permission to spend a weekend taking a break, climbing into bed with our favorite comfort food, and diving into our favorite cheesy novel without feeling like there is some other busywork that we should be doing instead.

Save the excuses that you cannot do anything about your overwork situation because your job, your boss, or your corporate culture wouldn't allow it. There is something you can do right now to make your situation better.

If you are not comfortable turning off your work cell phone during the weekend, then commit to checking your email only during designated times, instead of responding to your alert tones like one of Pavlov's dogs. If you can't have lunch away from your desk every day, at least do it once a week. If you can't meditate and relax for thirty minutes every day, then close your eyes and meditate for three minutes.

Excuses will not serve us during this movement. When it comes to respecting ourselves, we can *always* do something.

Again, there is a huge risk in doing nothing.

Don't wait until you're near death to come to this realization. Don't wait until someone close to you dies unexpectedly to come to this realization. Don't wait until your kid grows up without really knowing you, your significant other leaves you, your parents pass away, or your friends no longer return your calls to come to this realization. Don't wait until you suffer from a devastating health condition that could have been prevented if you took better care of yourself.

The universe has a funny way of helping us realize what's really important, and, unfortunately, some of those methods can be less than pleasant. Trust me on this.

Making our workplace work will require you to find the courage to draw a line in the sand that clearly says you will not be the next American workplace statistic. There is a better way. We can reject the glorification of busywork, we can consistently honor our priorities and boundaries, and, most of all, we can connect deeply with the people who matter to us the most while we are alive and able to do so.

To be relentlessly respectful and kind to others, we must be willing to be relentlessly respectful and kind to ourselves.

We cannot give what we don't have.

R.E.A.L. WORK
Assignment #3:

Determining Priorities, Setting Boundaries, and Drawing the L.I.N.E.

There is no hope of maintaining this movement without being clear about two things: our priorities and our boundaries.

As a reminder, our priorities are how we would like to focus our attention, energy, and time; and our boundaries are the limits that we create to protect those priorities.

For this assignment, write down your five top priorities *and* the boundaries that you will create to keep your priorities protected and safe. This exercise is the most important one in this book. It will ensure that you consistently honor yourself, while also ensuring that you do not allow yourself to be taken advantage of by anyone.

Additionally, find one area where you need to say no in your professional life, and use the L.I.N.E. (Listen, Inspect, NO, Enforce) strategy to say no with grace, while saying yes to yourself and your priorities.

Bonus assignment:

Write down one energy-renewing activity that you are committing to put into practice immediately. Whether it is getting at least eight hours of sleep a night, meditating daily, getting a massage once a month, exercising regularly, or taking regular vacations—choose something, and stick to it. The old model of expending your energy until you collapse or have a nervous breakdown is not a useful pursuit. On the other hand, focusing on the renewal of your energy is the new model to ensure that you always bring your best self to your work, and to your life. Your health, happiness, and ability to keep pushing this movement forward depend on you making the correct choice.

SECTION

3

THE LIFEBLOOD

Endless Energy

CHAPTER

7

THE FIGHT YOU MUST WIN

Developing an Unstoppable Attitude

The last of human freedoms—to choose one's attitude in any given set of circumstances, to choose one's own way.

—VIKTOR FRANKL

Nothing meaningful can be built without a foundation, and that work has been done.

We know that we can make the greatest positive impact in the workplace through our interpersonal skills and our ability to bring out the best in others. We know that taking ownership of our professional journey is the only way to control the outcome. We know that if we do not relentlessly respect ourselves by protecting our priorities and our time, we are destined to become the next burned-out American workplace statistic. Everything from this point forward will be built with these three foundational ideas in mind.

But what now?

Building on this solid foundation, we still need to do a lot more to complete this job. Here's where the movement to positively improve the workplace becomes exponentially harder. Somehow we have to tap into something within us that will keep us going when all seems hopeless and meaningless and when it would be much easier to quit.

To make this movement a reality, we must add a second layer to this process.

Energy.

Energy is defined as the capacity to do work. Without it, we cannot continue the movement by building on the foundation we created. Many people will give up here because they won't be able to push past the challenges that are waiting for us ahead.

You cannot be one of those people. We need you, Solutionist, because we are in a fight to maintain our energy to keep moving forward. Contrary to what some people might believe, this fight is not against difficult coworkers, micromanaging bosses, or unmanageable deadlines. *This is about winning the fight that is raging between our own two ears.*

The prize for winning this fight is an attitude that will propel us toward our objective of a more positive workplace, instead of pushing us further away from it.

We cannot afford to lose.

TRANSCENDING NEGATIVE CIRCUMSTANCES

There is something I know about you.

You have drama in your life. Don't worry, you are not alone—I have drama, too. Everyone does. Here is an even more depressing piece of information: No matter how positive, kind, and respectful you are, you cannot immunize yourself from the world's problems.

Drama does not care if you volunteer at your church, feed the homeless during your free time, or donate half of your biweekly paycheck to a shelter for abused animals. It will find you. Drama will drop lazy and self-serving coworkers in your path when you need help the most, crash your hard drive when you need to meet a rapidly approaching deadline, and leave you with a blank brain just moments before you need to give the presentation of your career for your company's senior leadership. And those are only our workplace problems.

What happens when your child dies, you suffer a huge financial setback and you are suddenly struggling to make ends meet, or you develop a life-altering illness?

The struggle is real. But as brutal as these circumstances are, they do not necessarily undermine a person's ability to keep moving forward in a positive direction.

I personally know of people who have lost a child to death, lost their homes to foreclosure, and lost their health to cancer, but they were all somehow able to transcend their devastating circumstances and continue to live their best lives, despite suffering debilitating setbacks. I am sure you know people in your life who have shown the ability to do the same. Maybe you yourself are one of those people.

Circumstances are not the determining factor in our ability and willingness to keep pushing forward. Some people give up despite seemingly having it all—fame, fortune, influence, good looks, and perfect health. Some people experience dire circumstances (the death of a loved one, an accident, or a disability) and they transcend those circumstances and go on to do amazing things.

It is their attitude that makes the difference.

So what is an attitude anyway?

I define it as our habitual way of thinking. Just like anything in life, we can have it work for us or against us. Your attitude determines how everything in your life will turn out—your career, your relationships, your health, your future success and happiness. *Literally, everything.* Your attitude is like food for your soul. The better the food, the better your body runs. The better your attitude, the better your soul runs. By default, the better your career will run, too.

If you don't have the right attitude, it could negatively affect your career and every relationship you have from this point forward. It is deeper than plastering a toothy grin on your face 24/7, screaming to the world about your positive attitude. We cannot make our workplaces work without understanding this: *The key to living a positive life is the ability to transcend negative circumstances.*

Here are the three steps to transcending negative circumstances:

Step 1: Acknowledge the reality of your situation. There is nothing positive or healthy about deluding yourself into believing that a toxic work environment is like a day trip to the spa. I cannot say this enough: Delusion and lying to yourself are not positivity.

Step 2: Realize that you have the power to improve the situation, your response to the situation, or both.

Step 3: Take action to do so.

In summary, the person who is controlled by negative circumstances responds by saying, "Ugh, this sucks." The person who transcends negative circumstances says, "This sucks, and I will find a way to make it better."

This is not magic. These are the only three steps every person who has overcome negative circumstances has taken.

Owning this attitude is not just the difference between success and failure in the workplace. It is the difference between happiness and misery, strength and weakness, and, dare I say, life and death.

The good news for us is that we can make the right choice whenever we are ready.

THE CHOICE: A TALE OF TWO CASHIERS

Last year during the holidays, my friend and I went into a nearby coffee shop and we experienced the power of choosing your attitude in action. It was extra busy in this particular coffee shop because they had just started serving their seasonal pumpkin-flavored goodies and drinks that everyone loves.

Then all of sudden, the cash registers stopped working and all hell broke loose. So much for the holiday spirit.

A visibly stressed-out manager came out from the back of the shop and split the growing mass of people into two lines, leading to separate cash registers. She apologized profusely for the inconvenience and then went back to fixing the cash registers.

At this point, my friend and I were split up and placed in two different lines, and we had two *very* different experiences.

Once I reached the register, I was face-to-face with a cashier who looked like he would rather be waterboarded for the rest of his shift than deal with another customer.

In a confrontational tone, he said to me, "Do you have cash?"

Apologetically, and caught totally off guard, I said, "Uh . . . no, I'm sorry. Just my credit card."

For a moment he looked as if he wanted to punch me in the mouth for being the latest thoughtless customer to inconvenience him, but instead he sighed, turned his back to me, and yelled to the back, "Susan, we have another card! I need more carbon paper!" Then he mumbled to himself, "Seriously, someone just shoot me now . . ."

"You know what, forget it. I'm good." And I left.

I was waiting outside when my friend came bouncing out of the coffee shop with her drink and her trademark smile.

"Where's your drink?" she asked.

I shared my tale of woe with her, and then she said, "That's strange. My cashier was *amazing.* She kept the mood light by promising to make us each the best drink we have ever had because of the inconvenience. She even pulled out a piece of notebook paper and asked each of us what was the most original thing that we wanted for the holidays. At the top of the list she wrote that she wanted a new cash register. It was so cute. She made a bad situation into an awesome one. I was the third customer in a row to give her a huge tip."

Think about this for a moment. Here were two cashiers placed in an identical situation: facing a line of annoyed customers with only a broken cash register in between them. One cashier had everyone in the line laughing and smiling and leaving her huge tips. The other cashier left the customers feeling even more annoyed than they were after waiting in line for fifteen minutes. That is, if they didn't end up walking out on him first, as I did.

Attitude was the only difference. The second cashier transcended a broken cash register by following the three steps of a positive attitude: She acknowledged that the situation was not ideal, she realized that she had the power to do something about it, and she did.

This is not even the end of the story.

A few days later, I went back to the same coffee shop and Mr. Grumpy Pants was working the cash register again. The shop was relatively empty, so I decided to engage him in conversation.

"I'm glad to see that the cash registers are working again," I said.

"Yeah, that was the worst day ever—these cash registers suck. When crap like that happens, I can't help it—I get so pissed off and

I can be an asshole to people. I got a few complaints from customers and my manager had to talk to me about it, but she doesn't get it. It's who I am, man. Know what I mean?"

"Actually, I don't. What you described doesn't have to be 'who you are.'"

"What are you talking about? It *is* who I am."

"It doesn't have to be. Once you become aware of this behavior, it immediately ceases to be an automatic reaction and it becomes something else—a choice. You don't have to act like that whenever the cash register goes down. You are *choosing* to act like that. Big difference, man."

He glared at me with the same look he had given me a few days earlier when I only had a credit card instead of cash, "Right. Just give me your order."

My response was the same this time, too.

"You know what, forget it. I'm good." And I left. The only difference between then and now is that I haven't been back since.

GOING VIRAL: THE ATTITUDE STRAIN

Like viruses, attitudes are contagious and it is worth examining if ours are worth catching.

The cashier in the coffee shop was not ready to hear the message because he had an attitude problem. Whether he understood it or not, his negative attitude spread like a virus throughout his line, and the resulting infections caused avoidable problems for him and his customers. On the flip side, the other cashier had the same success infecting the people in her line but with a much better outcome.

Let's think of the first cashier as a cautionary tale for us. We cannot improve our lives, least of all our workplace issues, if we have the yoke of an attitude problem hanging around our necks.

When you think of a person with an attitude problem in your workplace, be honest: Do you consider that person to be happy, successful, and living a life that you admire? Is this a person you would want to spend a minute of your free time around? Do you feel sad and disappointed when this person leaves a room you are in?

If you're like me, the answer is a resounding no. To make this movement succeed, we cannot repel people or, worse, compound the problems that we are working to transcend.

Unlike other pursuits, even if we are committed to maintaining a positive attitude, it can be very difficult to inoculate ourselves from the virus of negativity.

According to an article published by *Cleveland Clinic Wellness*, each person has an average of sixty thousand thoughts a day, 95 percent of which are the same thoughts repeated every day, and, on average, 80 percent of those habitual thoughts are negative.[1] That should terrify you. Tell me if any of these thoughts have crept through your mind during an average workday:

> *I work with a bunch of idiots. I feel dumber each minute I spend with these fools.*
>
> *They don't pay me enough to deal with this crap.*
>
> *This woman is giving me an attitude because I'm asking her to simply do her job? Really???*
>
> *I don't want to give this presentation. I know I'll screw it up, just as I did last time.*
>
> *This job is a like a recurring nightmare. I hate every millisecond of my life that I spend at this dump.*
>
> *What's the point in even trying? Nothing will ever change.*
>
> *Why do these things always happen to me?*
>
> *I can't stand this guy. I am ready to clock out and meet this punk in the parking lot for some good ol' fashioned street justice.*
>
> *My coworker's laugh is* so *annoying. It sounds like a hyena being skinned alive with a cheese grater.*
>
> *I am a terrible parent because I'm always at the office and not with my child.*

As if battling these thoughts weren't hard enough, it is about to get harder. In many cases, you might have to spend the majority of your waking hours at a job with people who constantly dump their negative attitudes on you. They may be on your work team, they may share a cubicle wall with you, or it might even be your boss. It is going to take some serious intestinal fortitude to deal with this on a daily basis.

Had enough? Sorry, there's more.

After you finally leave work and try to unwind, if you turn on the news or peruse social media, your brain will suffer an unrelenting assault of everything that is wrong with you, your community, your country, and the world. After repeatedly consuming a daily mental dose of wars, terrorism, rapes, murders, financial collapse, the latest political drama, and how you are not nearly as pretty or handsome as you thought you were, it is amazing that you can find the positivity to keep moving forward in any way.

Worst of all, our brains are hardwired to react more intensely to negative events than positive ones. The term *negativity bias* refers to the notion that negative stimuli have a greater and more sustained effect on our psychological state than equally weighted positive stimuli.

If you're keeping track, the negative voices are in our heads, they are surrounding us at work, and they're even shouting at us when we try to relax in front of the TV once the workday is done. There is no escape! On and on, the negative thoughts continue to infect our brains, our workplaces, and our personal lives until we unconsciously become a soldier of negativity ourselves.

Okay, enough of the bad news. Here's the good news.

Even though all of this is true, it hasn't changed one critical fact: *We will always remain in control of our attitudes.*

I cannot control how you think. Your boss cannot do it. The media can't do it, either. Only you can. Until the day you die, this is the most powerful weapon that you will ever possess in the battle against negativity at work or anywhere else on earth.

While we control our own thoughts, we shouldn't underestimate what we are up against in the fight to maintain a positive attitude. It is even more important to have strategies in place when keeping a positive attitude becomes immensely challenging.

Opposite is the Attitude Adjustment Pyramid. Like the world-famous Maslow Hierarchy of Needs, the Attitude Adjustment Pyramid has levels. Once you master the first level, you can move onto the next level until you eventually reach the top and become a self-actualized attitude ninja.

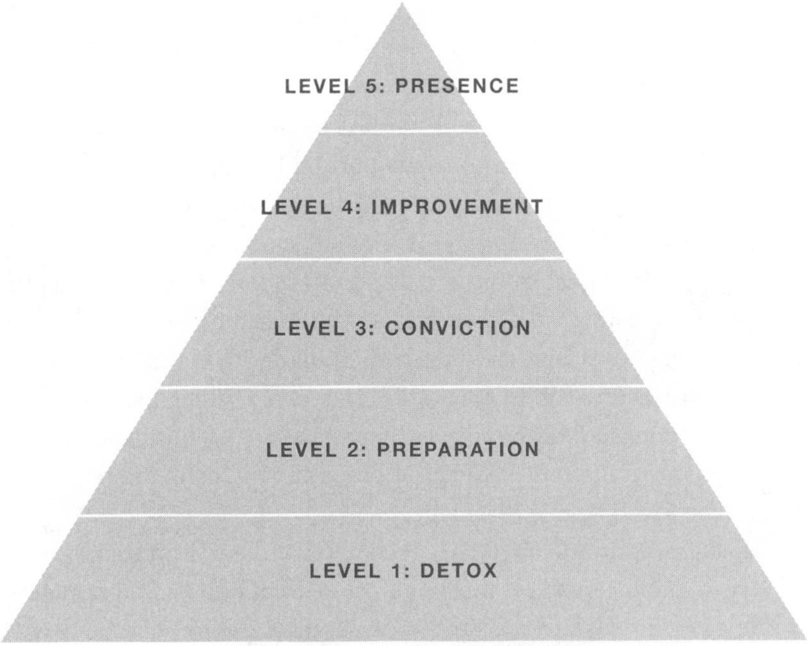

ATTITUDE ADJUSTMENT PYRAMID

So how can you protect yourself from negativity and sustain the energy to keep moving forward? Here's how.

Level 1—Detox: Taking Out the Trash

The first step on the Attitude Adjustment Pyramid is to do whatever you can to eliminate—or at least drastically limit—the negative influences in your life.

This step is critical.

Your attitude is your most prized possession because it literally determines your success or failure in every area of your life, and it is the one thing that will allow you to make the most meaningful contribution to the world. If you have friends, family members, or significant others who are making it harder for you to maintain your positive attitude and sanity, why would you keep them around? Making the workplace work is going to be hard enough without *voluntarily* dragging along people for the ride who are only compounding the pain, drama, and misery in your daily life. Just as cancer will wreak havoc on your body if left unchecked, the same will happen to your attitude if you keep these people in your inner circle, unchecked.

Does that sound ruthless? I hope it does.

This is not a game. This is serious business we're dealing with here. Ask yourself this about every personal relationship you are in right now: Does this relationship enrich my life or does it leave me feeling drained? If you answered "drained" and you are still choosing to keep that relationship in your life because you don't want to hurt that person's feelings, that's on you. Own the fact that you have made maintaining your positive attitude much harder than it needs to be.

The alternative is to lovingly move away from these relationships and choose healthier ones that sustain you and give you the energy to move forward, instead of doing the opposite. Some people need to be loved from a distance.

Just as important, if watching the news and being on social media all day is making you feel miserable, cynical of others, and hopeless, find something else to do. Read a book, take a walk, hang out with your kids, or go to the gym.

Personally, I do not watch the news very often.

Contrary to popular belief, avoiding the news doesn't make me less well informed than anyone else. Instead, it allows me to keep my attitude in check and be a more effective member of society. If something momentous is going on in the world or in my community, trust me, I'll find out about it as quickly as any news addict.

But, for me, it doesn't make any sense to load up my brain with a steady diet of kidnappings, terrorism, and murders every morning before I start my workday in hopes of "staying informed."

To keep up the energy to make sustained positive change, we have to own our attitude. And for us to be operating at maximum capacity, we can't afford to feed our attitude junk food or immerse it in toxins.

Once you have cleaned out the toxic relationships and influences that are within your control, it is time to move on to the next step.

Level 2—Preparation: Expect a Challenge

If you are in a situation in which you cannot immediately remove a toxic influence for whatever reason (say, it's your coworkers or your boss), you are going to need to shift your thinking.

The second level of the Attitude Adjustment Pyramid describes that shift as expecting a challenge. This simple shift can be a game-changer because it will also give you the energy to keep going when you feel like doing just the opposite.

I used to be a person who wanted everything to be easy. *My boss should be a better communicator! Why are my coworkers so damn rude and inconsiderate? This organization allows people to get away with murder—what kind of clowns are running this place?*

These thoughts, and many others like them, did nothing to change the objective reality of my situation. Instead, these thoughts just weakened my resolve and attitude and kept me stuck in place.

Since I expected things to be easy and to happen in a certain way, I was completely thrown off balance when things didn't go according to plan. And, in my plan, I didn't account for challenges, bumps in the road, and other inconveniences that are an unavoidable part of life. So when they unexpectedly showed up, I thought of them as huge, insurmountable barriers.

But what if we expected this process to be hard? What if we did not walk into this movement with blinders on and we expected to face challenging bosses, shady coworkers, and toxic work environments along the way? Just being aware that these barriers *could* come up lessens their power over us, because those barriers have lost the element of surprise. Expecting challenges will keep us prepared and ready to deal with them when they arise. Instead of being shocked at the appearance of a barrier, we are prepared for it because we knew it was coming. The actor Will Smith said it best: "If you stay ready, you ain't gotta get ready."

To be clear, this is not the same thing as saying, "I just expect the worst all the time, so if something good happens, I'm pleasantly surprised." Losers think that way. This is about expecting the best, while being prepared to deal with the worst. Instead of staying inside and doing nothing because you think it might rain, you are choosing to confidently step outside to enjoy your day, taking an umbrella with you, just in case.

Work, like life, can be hard. And isn't that how it should be? Making a meaningful change is not easy. We should expect a challenge when we are trying to improve our workplace and maintain our positive attitude. We should expect a fight for the life we deserve.

And we should expect to win while we're doing it.

Level 3—Conviction: Values over Emotions

Removing toxic influences and preparing for challenges are very helpful. But if we are unable to manage our emotions when we deal with the issues that are lurking in the workplace, we are in big trouble.

Level 3 of the Attitude Adjustment Pyramid is all about controlling our emotions through conviction.

The choice is a simple one—either you are in charge of your emotions or your emotions are in charge of you. I can confidently say that I have never met a person who has made a significant, positive, long-term difference in the workplace without having firm control over his or her emotions (and if you know someone who has, I'd be willing to bet that he could have done much more if he'd learned how to manage his emotions more effectively).

That is why values are so important. Instead of allowing our emotions to take control of our lives and constantly staying in a reactive state, we can choose to become crystal clear about our values, and then commit to living those values on a daily basis.

Our values reflect the core of who we are. These are the ideals that represent the most meaningful aspects of how we live and work. They are the parts of ourselves that we are unwilling to compromise. Here are the top three life values that guide me:

1. **Kindness:** I will be kind and respectful to others, regardless of what is happening around me or within me. I will not allow my mood to determine my manners. I am a kindness extremist.

2. **Self-Control:** I always have the power to determine my response to anything. I will not cede that power by allowing anyone else to influence my happiness, my peace of mind, or my sanity.

3. **Honor:** I will always be the man that my mama and daddy raised me to be (I'm a forty-one-year-old man, and that value will never change until the day I die).

I cannot overstate the power of having values, because they will keep you grounded in sanity when your emotions are hell-bent on sending you in the opposite direction. Am I perfect when it comes to choosing my values over my emotions? No, and you won't be either—thankfully, perfection is not the goal. The goal is to consciously bring your best self to your biggest challenges, as often as possible. Your values help you to do that. They will keep you moving forward and focused on solutions when the world is trying to distract you from what really matters. Most of all, they will keep you in a position to always create positive outcomes, even when you don't believe that a positive outcome exists.

My question for you is this: What do you value?

What is the changeless part of you that no one can mess with? What are the best aspects of you that you have demonstrated in the past, and are willing to demonstrate again, once the going gets tough? Are they self-discipline, friendliness, excellence, loyalty, ambition, service to others, consistency, never-ending improvement, grit, peace, humility, teamwork, integrity, hard work, enthusiasm, faith, self-control, focus, joy, leading by example, reliability, empathy, honor, fairness, positivity, something else?

Without thoughtful attention to this step in the Attitude Adjustment Pyramid, you are at heightened risk of getting emotionally hijacked the next time you are on the wrong end of some drama at work.

We can do better than being mindlessly reactive or, worse, dealing with all our problems by fighting fire with fire. Seriously, have you ever seen a firefighter run into a burning house while holding a flamethrower?

Fire cannot put out fires any more than drama can put a stop to drama. Water stops fires, and while our values don't stop drama, our values ensure that we respond to drama in a way that is in line with the core of who we are.

Live your values with conviction and lean on your values when your attitude is tested.

Level 4—Improvement: Making the Workplace Better than You Found It

At level 4 we move past responding to other people and focus on the attitude needed to proactively create a positive workplace environment.

This might sound simple, but the easiest way to make your workplace a better place is to commit to leaving everything better than you found it. It doesn't matter how small the act is, either. The only thing that matters is that you are doing something—anything—to make it better than it was before you arrived.

Here are a few of literally millions of potential examples:

- Smile at a stranger.
- Refill the coffeepot and/or the copier cartridge when they are empty.
- Resist the urge to spread gossip, mean-spiritedness, and other mindless negativity.
- Commit to performing a random act of kindness.
- Offer support or encouragement to a colleague who is having a difficult day.
- Give someone a sincere compliment.
- Support someone's idea instead of telling her why it can't be done.

You don't have to wait for someone else to do any of these things or, worse, choose to do nothing because you know that no one else at your workplace is willing to do this for you. It does not matter if anyone else is doing it. *All that matters is for you to do it.* And you are very capable of doing all those things right now.

If you don't know how you can leave something better than you found it, here is a simple question to ask yourself:

What can I do right now that would be helpful?

Helpfulness always makes any situation better, and if your attitude is locked in on finding ways to help others, you are officially making your workplace, and the world, a much better place.

Whether it is picking up a piece of stray trash or offering a kind word to a colleague who just got chewed out by an abusive customer, use this as your daily self-imposed attitude challenge:

> ***I will leave everything I touch and every person I meet a little better than I found them.***

Level 5—Presence: Just Today

Once we have mastered the four previous levels of the Attitude Adjustment Pyramid, we can finally move onto the final, and most powerful, level.

The fight to protect our attitude is not a fight that we need to win every day for the rest of our lives. We only have to win the fight today. Just today.

Remove the negative influences in your life? You can do it just today. Expect challenges at work and be prepared to deal with them? You can do that just today. Choose your values over your emotions? You can do that just today. Leave everything you touch better than you found it? Yes, you can do that just today, too.

There is no doubt in my mind that if we shift our focus to simply doing what we can do today, we'll be able to accomplish much more than we ever imagined.

Do you have to do all this tomorrow, too? Who cares? Tomorrow is irrelevant because it is not here yet. This is only about doing the right thing until we fall asleep tonight—and we can do *anything* today. As for tomorrow, we will deal with it when it gets here.

But when tomorrow eventually becomes today, we know what we need to do.

For now, there's only one day that matters, there's only one day that's real, and there's only one day when we must honor ourselves and our attitudes by giving our best effort consistently.

Just today.

R.E.A.L. WORK

Assignment #4:

Climbing the Pyramid

To sustain the energy needed to build our workplace positivity movement, we must maintain the right attitude. For this assignment, we'll forge our unstoppable attitude by systematically climbing each step of the Attitude Adjustment Pyramid.

Level 1—Detox: Taking Out the Trash

Write down on a piece of paper the people you voluntarily keep in your inner circle (friends, family members, significant others). Once you have listed everyone, simply determine if they either enrich your life the majority of the time (mark with a check mark) or if they drain you the majority of the time (mark with an **x**).

The ones who you marked with an **x** need to be cut out of your life ASAP or, at the very least, you must commit to drastically reducing your time with them. This process does not have to be overcomplicated and you are not being cruel by taking this action—this is solely about being kind to yourself. This also goes for any other draining influences in your life, like excessively watching TV news or Internet news feeds, for instance. List those draining influences and, for each one, list an alternative behavior that can be done in its place (such as listening to a motivational podcast, going for a walk, or calling a friend) Your attitude needs all the positive energy it can get, so commit to making today the day you stop feeding it mental and emotional junk food.

Level 2—Preparation: Expect a Challenge.

What challenges are lurking in your workplace? You might not know every single one, but chances are you know most of them. Just the act of listing them puts you in a more controlled state of mind because they can no longer surprise you. Take a moment to write down your workplace challenges so that you will be better prepared to deal with them when they inevitably show up in your life.

Level 3—Conviction: Values over Emotions.

What are your values? What are the unshakable and changeless parts of your core that make up who you truly are? If you don't know the answer to those questions, now is the time to figure it out and write it down. Your values are what will keep you from being hijacked by your emotions when things get rough.

Level 4—Improvement: Making the Workplace Better Than You Found It.

There are few better attitudes than one of helpfulness. What can you commit to do that will help make everyone and everything you touch better than you found them? Write down at least three helpful things you are willing to do consistently, and then do them. Don't wait for anyone else to make the positive change in your workplace that you are more than capable of doing yourself.

Level 5—Presence: Just Today.

Make a simple daily practice (I do this while brushing my teeth morning and night) of reminding yourself that you need to maintain your positive attitude just for today. While it is very easy to fall into the trap of obsessing over the past or fearing for the future, use your "just today" mantra to keep you focused on the present.

CHAPTER

8

YES, YOU'RE HERE TO MAKE FRIENDS:

Building Relationships That Last

If you want to go fast, go alone. If you want to go far, go together.

—AFRICAN PROVERB

"I'm not here at work to make friends."

What is the first response that enters your mind when you read the quote in the previous line? Before you answer, allow me to add some context.

In one of my first jobs after college, a colleague of mine (let's call her Nicole) returned to work after having her second miscarriage in a row. She and her husband had been trying to have a baby for a number of years, and this latest setback was understandably devastating to her. Thankfully, she had a group of coworkers who were there for her on her first day back at work to support her, provide emotional comfort when needed and simply help her make it through the day.

That's what friends are for, right?

Wrong. At least, it was according to my former supervisor.

The supervisor in question (let's call him Jack) had no interest in offering any emotional support to our returning coworker. I am not suggesting that he had to envelop her in a warm embrace all day, but at a minimum, an acknowledgment of her situation would have been a decidedly human thing to do, considering the circumstances.

In a move that was as shocking as it was cruel, Jack walked over to Nicole's desk while she had her head in her hands and coldly said, "Welcome back. This work isn't going to handle itself, so you should get your act together and get started." He then dumped a pile of work on her desk that made a loud thud and then remorselessly walked back into his office.

Jack was notoriously difficult to work for. He rarely acknowledged anyone's efforts, he only spoke to people when he needed something, and he could quite possibly be one of the most unapproachable people I have had the misfortune of dealing with in any workplace.

While that was all true, after seeing how shaken Nicole was by Jack's behavior, I could not just sit there and pretend that nothing had happened. I am not a confrontational guy by nature, but something propelled me into Jack's office and I asked him why he had been so rude to Nicole. Here was his memorable response:

"Look, I'm not here at work to make friends. I'm here to do my job and make sure that all of you do yours."

I know that some people will side with me on this—to me, that was unnecessarily cold. Other people might think that is a reasonable thing for a supervisor to say. If you fall in the latter camp, read on, because this chapter was written with you in mind.

THE CAREER-SAVING IMPORTANCE OF FRIENDSHIP

With the possible exception of "The customer is always right," the saying "I'm not here to make friends" is the most outdated and destructive saying in business today.

A friend is simply someone you like and respect. Based on that definition, wouldn't you want to make sure that you had as many friends as humanly possible at work or anywhere else? It is not a controversial stance to say that anyone who cares about creating a more positive and productive work environment must be focused on making friends at work.

Let's break this down mathematically. The average American works forty hours a week, for forty-nine weeks a year (subtracting three weeks a year for holidays, vacations, and sick days). That's a total of 1,960 working hours a year. If you maintain that average from the time you graduate from college (at twenty-two years old) until retirement (at age sixty-five), that's a grand total of 84,280 working hours in a lifetime. Seriously, just consider that number for a moment. That is *a lot* of hours. Since this is the case, shouldn't it be a priority to spend the majority of that time with people you like and respect?

Jack didn't see it that way, and he viewed the "friends at work" idea very differently. To him, having a friend at work meant that you had someone to slack off with, and friendship only got in the way of productivity, instead of enhancing it. Drawing on his old-school mentality, his two favorite go-to sayings were "Put your head down, shut your mouth, do your work, and then go home" and "If you have time to chat with a coworker, you don't have enough work to do."

Even worse, he used his "I'm not here to make friends" attitude as an excuse not to be kind or respectful to anyone. He would raise his voice constantly, he didn't care enough to get to know the names of all the people on his team (he would constantly call me "Shilo"), and he only spoke to people when he needed something from them. It was as if he viewed employees as expendable pieces of chewing gum. He would maniacally chomp every last ounce of flavor out of all the employees, spit them out, and then curse at the wads of gum on the ground for not providing any more value. Not surprisingly, everyone hated him.

Rejecting the importance of building meaningful relationships in the workplace is a career-limiting move. Jack never understood that in the brief time I worked for him. Not only did people consciously and intentionally choose not to work hard for him, but his attitude led to a great deal of miscommunication, absenteeism, and lots of other needless interpersonal drama because people did not feel comfortable speaking with each other. His lack of interest in building relationships made people less productive and worse at their jobs.

Jack is not an isolated example. Throughout my career, I have encountered hundreds of people (some were even well-intentioned) who largely dismissed the idea of the workplace as an appropriate place for friendship.

And, just like Jack, many of them greatly limited their professional success because of it.

I don't want that for you.

"IF YOU WANT TO GO FAR, GO TOGETHER"

The African proverb at the beginning of this chapter is so simple, and yet so brilliant: "If you want to go fast, go alone. If you want to go far, go together." Jack and others like him may go fast, but they cannot go far alone.

Friendship is a key ingredient in maintaining the energy needed to go as far as we can with this movement.

Friendship at work is important for countless reasons. According to research compiled by OfficeVibe.com, 70 percent of employees say that making friends at work is the most crucial factor in a happy working life, 50 percent of employees who had a best friend at work reported that they felt a strong connection with their company, and there is a 35 percent increase in the quality of work among people who have a best friend at work.[1]

But let's put the research aside for a moment, and focus on the purely human aspect of friendship. Isn't it easier to put forth your best effort, communicate openly and often, and fully support people you like and respect?

If nothing else, remember this key truth about friendship: *When people like you, they will help you.*

And, believe me, we are going to need help. In most careers, no one can be successful without the willing help of others. Here are three of the most common reasons this is true:

1. We will deal with rude and condescending people in the workplace, and we will need help to stay sane. Difficult people are found in every workplace—it could be an annoying

coworker, an abusive customer, or a micromanaging boss. These situations are very common. If you don't have a trusted friend with whom you can blow off steam or share a laugh when you feel like crying, difficult situations will become unbearable in a hurry.

2. You will work on projects with other people and you will need their help to ensure your success and the success of the team. People generally work harder for someone they like and respect, even if the sole motivator is that they don't want to let their friends down.
3. Most of all, just like my former coworker Nicole who miscarried, life will pull the rug out from under you without warning, and you will need someone who is there to help you get through it. Life happens while you are working—loved ones may die, you may get divorced, your kids may get injured at school, you may develop cancer, you may get into a car accident. Hardships are an inevitable part of the human experience and no one is tough enough to deal with the pain alone. You need support during those times. Even though Jack was unwilling to provide any comfort to Nicole, many of her workplace friends supported her when she needed it the most. I doubt that she would have made it through that day without them.

We cannot go through our lives alone, so how can we go through our careers alone? Friends provide us with the energy to keep going when the thought of another day at work sounds as appealing as contracting a stubborn case of head lice. Finding as many people as possible we like, respect, and trust in the workplace should be the number-one priority for anyone reading this book.

If you are ready to create lasting friendships at work and build your own Solutionist Society, here are two simple truths worth remembering.

1. You Have to Own It before You're Shown It

I'm not a dating expert, but humor me for a moment.

How many times have you heard the same tired advice given to single people about attracting their ideal mate into their lives? You have heard it yourself, too, I'm sure. We should write a list of all the key personality traits we would like to see in our ideal mate in hopes of becoming crystal clear on who we want to show up in our lives.

Makes sense, right? I used to think so, too. But not anymore.

My advice to single people is slightly different. Yes, if you are single, you should write down the key traits that you are looking for in a mate, but once you are done making that list, you need to go out and *live every single one of those traits, consistently.*

In other words, just like everything in life, we need to own the traits we want to see in others before others show those traits to us. How could we expect to attract the people we want in our lives if we are unable or unwilling to live up to those same standards ourselves?

The workplace is no different.

If you are looking for more kindness to appear in your life at work, the ideal way to start is by being kind yourself. Volunteer to help others, be supportive of another coworker's goals, listen fully and actively, commit a random act of workplace kindness, or simply smile at a stranger in the hallway. Gandhi knew what he was talking about when he wisely said, "Be the change that you want to see in the world." We have the opportunity right now to do this in any workplace by being kind, honest, relentlessly respectful, and, most of all, positive. If you won't do it, who will?

It is not my style to overcomplicate an idea that does not need any extra complexity. If we simply express in our lives the standards we want to see in others, we will attract the right people into our work lives. It works without fail.

I have worked in some of the most toxic workplaces imaginable, and even as I nearly drowned in a noxious sea of backstabbers, bullies, and unrelenting negativity, I was able to make friends. In fact, the friends I made there are some of the best friends I have ever had. I might be dead without them.

I made those relationships by being the type of friend I wanted in my life. Did I run into a few people who mistook my kindness for weakness? Yes. That's part of life—I course-corrected, and found different people to connect with deeply, and I left those fake friends behind. But by being open and friendly, I found Solutionists (long before I even made up the term) who were willing to fight the good fight to make the workplace a more positive experience for themselves and for others.

I know this may be hard to believe if you are currently treading water in a sea of toxicity that is similar to the one I survived. But there's some very good news in the next section.

2. There Are More of Us

Statistics have shown that there are millions of people who want to experience a more positive version of work than they are experiencing now. I want to take a more controversial stance on this, though. Not only are you not alone in wanting to experience a more positive work environment, but also I believe there are *more people* who think that kindness and respect should be standard at every workplace, than there are people who think just the opposite.

The only question is this: Can you see it?

Believe it or not, I learned how to see this truth more clearly after watching the popular Pixar movie *A Bug's Life*. In this animated classic, the kind and gentle ants were relentlessly bullied and tormented by the bigger and stronger grasshoppers. The grasshoppers demanded that the ants gather food for them each season or risk getting squished by the grasshoppers. Each season it was the same thing over and over again until Flik, the protagonist in the movie, realized something.

There were more ants than grasshoppers. In fact, the ants outnumbered the grasshoppers one hundred to one. Once the ants were able to look past the grasshoppers' size, their loud voices, and their intimidating presence, the ants banded together and won.

That simple concept was burned into my consciousness the first time I watched that movie with my young daughters, and it has stayed with me ever since. I believe that the workplace is no different. Sure, the workplace asshats and jerks might talk tough, be well-connected, have powerful titles, and be world-class intimidators—but that does not change the truth.

There are more of us.

There will *always* be more people who believe in kindness and mutual respect in the workplace than those misguided souls who believe just the opposite. But we still need to be honest about what we're dealing with here. The current state of the American workplace is broken and, in many cases, the asshats and the bullies are the ones running the show. This battle is too dangerous to fight alone. You are going to need some help—scratch that, *we* are going to need some help—to make this movement successful. Until we finally band together and unite behind this shared vision of positivity at work, we will be squished just as any lone ant would be taking on a grasshopper.

Creating your Solutionist Society is a key step in making the workplace work.

Start with just one person. Find one person who will have your back, support you when times get tough, and who is willing to stand shoulder to shoulder with you as you lead by example. That is a real friend, and you are going to need as many of them as you can possibly find for this movement to succeed.

Your friends are out there, and they are waiting for you to find them.

CLIQUES: THE ANTIFRIENDSHIP

A quick word of warning: As you build your Solutionist Society, you could easily fall into the trap of making this movement worse, instead of better.

One reason that certain people are opposed to friendships at work is that, in some cases, friendships at work turn into cliques. And cliques don't make any workplace more positive.

A clique is a small group of people with shared interests who do not allow others to join them, and that is the antithesis of this movement. People who create cliques often build their group on the shaky foundation of gossip, mean-spiritedness, and exclusion. Being part of a group of people who cut themselves off from the rest of the department or company, in hopes of becoming the new workplace cool kids, is nothing more than a bizarre, ego-fueled exercise in stupidity. I have never known a clique that has positively changed the world.

If you feel that your Solutionist Society is devolving into a clique, get yourself back on track by asking these two questions:

1. **Do we spend more time talking about people or to people?** It is very naive to think that we will never talk about other people from time to time, but if that is *all* we are doing, we have lost sight of the purpose of this movement. Our goal is a simple one: to solve our workplace issues by creating a more positive experience at work. Gossip will not make that happen. If someone is the frequent target of your gossip sessions, why are you just talking about it? Wouldn't it make more sense to take action to make it better? Using up your discretionary time berating a person who is not even present to defend himself is not a useful practice.

   Also, if you are stuck in the habit of talking about people, I would highly recommend instituting Gossip-Free Fridays (feel free to designate any day of the week; I just happen to like doing this on Fridays). Choosing one day a week when you are not allowed to say anything negative about another person behind her back is such a simple, yet brilliant, exercise. I dare you to try it—you may be shocked at how much time you spend talking negatively about other people. Awareness is the first step when it comes to kicking any unhealthy habit, and once you try it for one day, you will want to do it more often.

2. **Are we exclusive or inclusive?** Solutionists are not an exclusive group. The purpose of this movement is to share it with as many people as humanly possible who are passionate about creating a kinder and more respectful workplace. We are not here to leave anyone out or behind—entry is open to anyone who is willing and able to do the work of creating a more positive workplace. The more the merrier.

WHAT FRIENDS ARE *REALLY* FOR

When I think about the benefits of having true friends at work, the camaraderie and the unfailing support when bad things inevitably happen are easiest to note. Both are extremely important, but there is still one additional positive benefit that I haven't mentioned yet.

> ***A real friend helps you to become the best version of yourself.***

When it would be much easier to quit than to take another step forward or when the temptation arises to fight other people's rudeness and negativity by being even ruder and more negative, your real friend won't let you go down that road.

Self-accountability is one of the three foundational skills of making the workplace work, and there can be no movement without being intimately connected to your Hire Self. However, there will be times when your energy level is low and the drama is high, and you will need help to keep yourself on track. During those times, having a friend who cares enough about you to hold you accountable could be the difference between success and failure.

The only prerequisites to choosing an accountability partner are (1) the person must sincerely care about doing whatever is possible to create a more positive workplace and (2) you are both willing to give each other honest feedback. If you have someone like that at work, you have found a true friend, and there is no limit to what you can do together.

Most of all, don't let anyone convince you that the workplace is not a place for friendship. We need friends so we can stay engaged, productive, and sane on a daily basis, and I don't believe that we can sustain any of those things in the workplace by ourselves.

Alone, we can only go fast, but together we can take this movement very far.

That's what friends are for.

R.E.A.L. WORK
Assignment #5:

Building a Society

This movement cannot succeed if only one person in a workplace is onboard. To maximize our impact, we will need to maximize our numbers; that is why building relationships is the linchpin of how we will make the workplace work.

This assignment is divided into two sections. Part One: If you do not have a friend at work, and Part Two: If you do have a friend (or friends) at work.

Part One: Find a Friend.

Reject the idea that you can create positive change in your workplace by stuffing headphones into your ears, and by avoiding eye contact and conversation with anyone unless absolutely necessary. If you work in an environment in which kindness, respect, and civility are absent, chances are there is someone who works with you who feels the same way you do. Start by simply reaching out to others by being the workplace friend you would like to have. Be supportive, be kind, be a good listener, be respectful, and, yes, be positive. If you work in a truly toxic environment, your attempts to be friendly may be rejected. That's okay. Dust yourself off and move on. Don't let yourself lose faith in humanity and retreat back to the safety of your headphones. There is someone in your workplace you can connect with, and finding that person will provide you with the strength and energy to keep going. Once you find that person, move onto Part Two.

Part Two: Meet Regularly.

Start by having a meeting with your work friend(s) (aka your Solutionist Society) and have all of them share with the group their relentless respect commitments, which you made in chapter 4. The purpose of this meeting is threefold: (1) to resolve to live out those commitments regardless of how others around you are acting; (2) to allow everyone in the group the freedom to lovingly call each other out and offer support if and when they fall short of the standards you created; and (3) to brainstorm if there is anyone else who would be willing to join your positivity movement. This is how positive change happens—by being the change that you want to see in the world, staying accountable for that change, and by finding as many people as possible who are willing to do the same. Ideally, your Solutionist Society will meet on a regular basis (weekly at the least, but preferably daily), even if it is only for a few minutes, to review the tools in this book (the Attitude Adjustment Pyramid, staying true to your Hire Self, drawing the L.I.N.E., and so on), to keep each other's spirits high, and to remain focused on continuous positive change. As motivational speaker Zig Ziglar once said, "People often say that motivation doesn't last. Well, neither does bathing—that's why we recommend it daily."

Use each meeting as a reminder to stop giving the most challenging people in our lives (our bullying bosses, our annoying coworkers, even our significant others) the sacred right to determine what we should be thinking or how we should be behaving. From now on, that level of influence is reserved solely for us and our Solutionist Society.

CHAPTER

9

A STARVING WORLD:

The Power of Appreciation

Next to physical survival, the greatest need of a human being is psychological survival, to be understood, to be affirmed, to be validated, to be appreciated.

—STEVEN COVEY

Undoubtedly, you have heard these familiar stories before:

The friend who is expected to always be there with money to lend, a shoulder to cry on, and a couch to crash on at a moment's notice whenever it's needed, but is not appreciated for doing so.

The wife who stays home with the kids and keeps the house spotless, but does not hear a word of thanks from her husband for her efforts because that is what stay-at-home parents are "supposed to do."

The son who went his entire life without hearing how much he was loved or appreciated by his father, until his dad's final moments before he died.

We are an appreciation-starved society. I personally know of many people who have ended marriages, harbored deep bitterness toward their parents, and walked away from lifelong friendships because of a lack of appreciation.

If a lack of appreciation can have such a destructive effect on relationships between two people who love each other, imagine what would happen in a workplace environment with people who may not even like or respect each other. Predictably, the results are devastating. Consider these statistics for a minute:

- The number-one reason most Americans leave their jobs is that they don't feel appreciated.[1]
- According to one study, 65 percent of people surveyed said that they did not receive any recognition for good work in the previous year.[2]
- Seventy-seven percent of employees said they would work harder if their efforts were better recognized and appreciated.[3]

The craziest part of all of this is that it does not cost a dime to do this well. You don't need to dip into your company's recognition tool kit and make it start raining gift cards. It doesn't even take a lot of time. This can be done in a matter of minutes, even seconds.

As the quote opening this chapter states clearly, being appreciated and validated is not a want. *It's a need.* We don't want oxygen, food, and water—we need them. The same goes for appreciation. Superstars need it, shy people need it, the CEO of your company needs it, you need it, and I need it. In the workplace, it is time to start thinking about appreciation as a life-sustaining necessity, rather than a life-enhancing luxury.

Without it, we have no hope of sustaining the energy needed to propel this movement.

So, if taking the time to appreciate our colleagues has the power to increase discretionary effort, stop the revolving door of turnover, make people feel better about the work they're doing, and provide the energy needed to keep pushing forward when things get tough, why in the world don't we do it more often?

There are four reasons.

1. We Don't Know We're Not Doing It

Most people wildly overestimate how much their thoughts, intentions, and mental states are known by others. In the world of psychology, this is known as the "illusion of transparency" and it can be a very sneaky enemy in creating a more positive workplace.

As a graduate student, Elizabeth Newton tested this phenomenon and reported her findings in her PhD dissertation for Stanford University.[4] She asked subjects to think of a well-known tune, such as "Happy Birthday" or "The Star-Spangled Banner." Then they were asked to tap out the tune with their finger on a table while another person (with no knowledge of the song chosen) listened carefully.

Before the tapper started tapping, he was asked what percentage of people would correctly guess the song that was being tapped. On average, the tappers guessed that 50 percent would be able to correctly guess the song being tapped. The reality? *Less than 3 percent could do it.*

What happened?

The tapper could hear the song clearly in his head as he tapped it out melodically on the table, and he naively assumed that everyone else would be humming along to the same tune—*except they weren't.* This theory was later tested by other researchers in other ways, ranging from subjects hiding their disgust when drinking a foul-tasting drink, to masking when they were lying to others. In every situation, the results were the same—people believed that their emotions were more obvious to others than they actually were.

What does this have to do with appreciation? Potentially everything.

What if you think that you've been doing a good job showing your appreciation for others, but in reality, you're expecting others to read your mind? You might *think* that Shannon in the Accounting Department knows how much you deeply appreciate her, but unless you've taken the time to tell her that, chances are she doesn't.

This is too important to be left to chance. While everyone else is figuratively tapping songs out on a table and assuming that everyone around them can read their minds, we must do something different:

- Make a regular point of sincerely saying "Thank you" to others on a daily basis.

- Catch people doing things right (more on this later in the chapter).

- Keep track in a journal, or a reminder app on your smartphone, of how often you actively express appreciation to others.

- Ask people to give you feedback on how well you are doing in showing your appreciation.

Your best intentions are great, but clear and meaningful action is much better.

2. We Don't Value It as Much as We Should

A few years ago, as I was conducting a leadership training class, I had a memorable exchange with a manager who had been in his role for seventeen years. I remember this because he kept proudly repeating how long he'd been a manager throughout the class, as if that somehow validated his leadership expertise. When I started to talk about the critical importance of appreciation in the workplace, it was clear that I struck a nerve with him, and he blurted out the following in front of the class:

> *"Are we really at the point where you want me to thank people for doing their damn jobs? This isn't tee-ball, where everyone gets a trophy, a pat on the back, and a smiley sticker simply for showing up. This is the real world, and if they want appreciation, they need to earn it."*

"So, what would be worthy of receiving sincere appreciation from you?" I asked with genuine curiosity.

I could sense his annoyance that I was challenging his opinion. "Something that matters, obviously," he said as his voice was beginning to rise. "Defusing a situation with an angry customer who is about to leave to join a competitor. Coming up with an idea that saves our department or company thousands of dollars. The stuff that matters."

"What about the employees who haven't had an opportunity to do those things, but they are regularly doing their jobs in an exemplary manner?" I asked again with continued curiosity.

He leaned back in his chair with a self-satisfied smirk. "That's just part of the job. If they're doing their jobs well, they should be hearing plenty of thanks from the customers. I don't have time to run around ass-patting my staff for doing what they're paid to do. I'm sorry if people don't like it."

Well, at least he apologized.

This is a prime example of a person who should not be entrusted with the responsibility of leading anyone. He later shared some incoherent ramblings about how praise makes people "complacent and soft" and that the job of a true leader is to consistently expose people's shortcomings so that they will be inspired to do better.

If you think he's alone in this belief, think again. Sadly, I have encountered hundreds of people who are like the manager in this story. According to a study conducted by the John Templeton Foundation, people are less likely to express gratitude at work than anyplace else.[5] In over a decade of working with corporate leaders from a variety of different industries, I have found numerous reasons for this. Usually, it is a combination of factors, including feeling that they will be taken advantage of if they express gratitude, feeling that focusing on what is wrong will achieve faster results than pointing out what is going well, and believing that expressing appreciation is a fuzzy, soft skill that gets in the way of real work. Not only is all that completely untrue, but also each time I have encountered a leader who believed in these falsehoods, his team inevitably underperformed in comparison to teams of leaders who recognized the value of appreciation.

Appreciating others is not only valuable, but it is also how we will make the workplace work. Is there anything more crucial in the workplace than maximizing the discretionary effort of the people around us? That is what sincere appreciation does. It builds confidence and self-esteem, it confirms that hard work and effort are acknowledged and recognized, it makes people feel that they are making a meaningful and positive difference, and most importantly, the behavior you reinforce through acts of appreciation will more likely be performed again in the future.

If a colleague helped you to defuse a situation with a difficult customer, thank him for it. If your boss gave you constructive feedback in a spirit of mutual respect and learning, thank her for it.

Appreciation is the key to creating a motivated, engaged, and energized workforce. To change the culture of workplace disengagement, it must be valued as the life-changing tool that it is. If you work in an environment in which appreciation is lacking, it is up to you bring the energy to this positivity movement by consistently and sincerely expressing appreciation.

Curing cancer, mapping the human genome, and single-handedly saving your company from financial ruin are not the only things worthy of receiving a thank-you. Withholding praise is the quickest way to destroy any relationship—personal or professional.

3. We're Doing It Wrong

One day at work, I received a knock on my office door from a manager who was looking for one of her employees.

"Hey, Shola, have you seen Michael?" the manager said half-heartedly.

"Nope, I haven't seen him all day," I replied as I finished typing up an email.

"Okay, thanks," she said as she slid an envelope under his closed office door and walked away.

An hour later Michael stormed into my office with a look of bewilderment and disgust on his face as he held the envelope in his hand.

"Shola, do you know what this is?" he said, with palpable anger hanging from his every word.

"I have no clue, man. Your boss slid it under your door a little while ago."

"It's a five dollar gift card. There's no note or anything. I don't even know what this is for. She couldn't even wait to look me in the eye and hand it to me in person? She just slid it under my door? Pathetic. I don't even want this crap." He promptly threw it in the trash as he walked away, sulking.

That is an example of appreciation done horribly wrong. What Michael's manager intended as an expression of recognition and appreciation had the exact opposite effect.

To authentically appreciate someone, you must express your appreciation in a sincere, specific, and meaningful way. Sliding a plastic gift card under a closed door fails miserably on all accounts.

Be Sincere

This is the easy part, but it's by far the most crucial. If you're known for walking into a room wildly slinging BS with both hands in the guise of appreciating people, they will be able to see it and smell it from a mile away. Don't insult them and embarrass yourself by engaging in anything less than sincere appreciation. If you're doing this, stop. You're not fooling anyone except yourself.

Be Specific

For appreciation to have maximum punch, it must be specific. Simply saying, "Hey Amber, thanks for last Thursday—that was awesome," isn't good enough. Most likely, as you walk away, she'll be thinking, *What in hell happened last Thursday?*

Instead, use her name, what she did, and why it mattered to you. For example:

"Hey, Amber, thank you so much for your willingness to help me whenever I have a question or a concern. Yesterday, when I called your department to ask you about a challenging issue that I've been dealing with, you took the time to walk me through it and address all my questions with patience and kindness. I feel so much more confident about dealing with these types of issues in the future because of the time you took with me yesterday. Thanks again, I really appreciate it."

Whoa.

That's a powerful expression of appreciation. The most beautiful thing is that this type of specific recognition will help to create a repeat performance. Just by taking the time to appreciate Amber you have motivated her to provide the same level of service with others in the future. Also, if you delivered that type of appreciation to Amber while others were within earshot, they will now know specifically what to do to receive that kind of praise, too.

Best of all, it's free and it only took between thirty and forty-five seconds to do it expertly.

Make It Meaningful

There are a lot of reasons that the pitiful attempt at appreciation by Michael's manager failed, but the main reason is that it wasn't meaningful. There is nothing meaningful about sliding a gift card under a closed door and walking away thinking you did something positive.

For appreciation to be meaningful, it should be thoughtful, creative, and personalized. There is no "one size fits all" method for showing appreciation, and those who truly make a positive difference in their workplaces recognize this.

This may take some trial and error, and that's okay. Genuinely making the effort to show appreciation in an environment in which it rarely exists is an exercise well worth the effort. For example, some employees would equate public praise to the joy of winning an Academy Award, while others would rather chew on broken glass than be recognized in front of their peers because it would embarrass them.

Here are some simple ways to give people meaningful recognition:

- Look them in the eye and point out how their actions have positively affected you.
- Make sure they are involved in decisions that affect their work.
- Make sure they feel genuinely heard.
- Listen to their suggestions about how a process can be improved at work.
- Explain how they have helped you while you're both at a team meeting (if appropriate).
- Write an email or, better yet, a handwritten note, expressing your appreciation.
- Treat the employee to lunch.

If you are unsure about how to show recognition to a colleague or boss, don't hesitate to ask. In the rare instance that someone is put off by your sincere, specific, and meaningful attempt to offer appreciation, don't let that stop you. More people will appreciate it than not appreciate it, if you are genuine.

While Michael's $5 plastic gift card is slowly decomposing in a landfill somewhere, meaningful appreciation can live on forever.

4. We're Not Doing It often Enough

"If people keep recognizing me for the hard work that I'm putting in here each day, I swear, I'm going to quit. I'm tired of this appreciation crap . . ."

Said by no one, ever.

When it comes to recognition and appreciation, no one's cup will ever be completely full. I have no problem admitting that the day will never come when I will be tired of hearing that my work is making a positive difference, and I believe that most people feel the same way about their efforts. That's why sincere appreciation must be a constant practice. Even if you follow all the steps already outlined in this chapter, you will fall short if you don't appreciate people often.

If we want to use appreciation as a tool to positively energize our workplaces, we cannot sit back and wait for events that are worthy of our appreciation to happen—we must actively focus on catching people doing things right. This is the mantra of the Solutionist. In a working world where people are solely focused on finding fault and mistakes, our ability to do the opposite will change the world.

So how often is enough? Every day.

Do not walk out of the workplace every day without taking the time to sincerely, specifically, and meaningfully appreciate someone. Remember the negativity bias that I cited in chapter 7? Positive stimuli do not stick in our minds for some reason, and that is why we need to keep introducing the stimulus of appreciation whenever it is appropriate.

The power of gratitude is infectious, and if you are the first to appreciate others, it will only be a matter of time before the attitude of gratitude spreads. Emotional contagion is real, and so is the power of appreciation. So why leave it to chance?

Even if it didn't spread, would you let that stop you from doing the right thing? Employees are under more stress than ever. Customers, colleagues, and bosses can reach you at all hours of the day and night via email or cell phone. Pressure to overdeliver is at an all-time high. Burnout is inevitable without the fuel of appreciation.

THE LIFE-CHANGING POWER OF APPRECIATION

As mentioned at the beginning of this chapter, studies have shown that the number-one reason most Americans quit their jobs is a lack of appreciation and recognition.

Unfortunately for you, the employee who is going to quit isn't the guy taking two-hour naps in the bathroom stall every afternoon after lunch. Trust me, he's happy and he isn't going anywhere. The people who are going to bail the most quickly are the most talented, well-trained, and hardest-working employees who desperately want to feel that their considerable skills and talents are appreciated.

This is very bad news for you. Why? Because the people who are making your job easier are the ones who are planning their exit strategies, while you're stuck working with the guy taking the infamous crap nap every afternoon—unless you do something about it.

When people's hard work is ignored, they start to wonder why they're working so hard in the first place. Maybe your boss or colleagues are unwilling to offer appreciation, but you can. And, as you already read in this chapter, it can be extremely simple to do.

That's what makes the concept of sincere appreciation so deeply moving and so profoundly sad. I have seen hundreds of people, including corporate executives, college athletes, and even police officers, shed a tear when someone looked them in the eye and sincerely told them how much they were appreciated.

Many years ago, during a particularly hard stretch for me at work, I came back to my desk and saw a sticky note from one of my colleagues. I had just finished enduring one of my boss's famous tirades, and on the note it simply said:

> *"Even though your boss may not see it, I think that you are sweet, smart, and a ray of sunshine during my cloudy days. I appreciate who you are, so please don't let her, or anyone, change who you are!"*

I kept that note for close to ten years and it sustained me whenever I felt sorry for myself. I read it when I felt there was no point in being the nice guy, standing up for kindness, or working toward a more civil workplace. That tiny little sticky note is one of the factors that prompted me to write this book.

Never underestimate the power of appreciation. It can literally change someone's life.

It changed mine.

R.E.A.L. WORK
Assignment #6:

Showing the Love

This assignment is about creating the habit of authentic appreciation. I want to challenge you in this area because I know how powerful this act can be in practice. Specifically, I want you to offer sincere, specific, and meaningful appreciation to someone at work for *thirty consecutive workdays.*

It does not matter who it is—it could be the parking lot attendant, your coworker, the cashier in the cafeteria, your boss, or someone from the executive team. I also don't care if you show your authentic appreciation to the same person each day (although, in order to maximize your positive impact, it would be much better to spread the appreciation around to as many different people as possible). The point is to do this for thirty straight workdays, with no exceptions. Also, don't rely on your memory to do this. Set a reminder on your smartphone or your computer each day to stop what you're doing and show the love.

Lastly, if you think you cannot do this sincerely for thirty straight days, you have proven why we have an appreciation problem in the first place. The best leaders—those with the most widespread positive impact—naturally and sincerely do this every day, and I know that anyone can get there, too, with deliberate practice. If you're paying attention to what is going on around you, you will easily be able to find something and someone to appreciate each day. And you will be shocked at how good you will feel by doing this. Not only will you positively change the people whose work you are appreciating, but also I am going on record saying that you yourself will be positively changed as well.

SECTION

4

THE COURAGE

Addressing the ABCs of Workplace Negativity

CHAPTER

10

DEALING WITH THE ABCs OF WORKPLACE NEGATIVITY

ABC #1: Asshats

I am thankful for all those difficult people in my life.
They have shown me exactly who I don't want to be.

—ANONYMOUS

Do you want to know what's really sad?

The fact that many people will likely see the title of this chapter in the table of contents and immediately head here first. No, I'm not sad that you skipped the first nine chapters. (I know you'll go back because you can't make the movement a success without them.) What makes me sad is that so many people in this world are stuck dealing with difficult people at work and they don't know how to deal with them.

My hope is that this chapter and the following two chapters will provide some much-needed relief and answers.

Relentless respect and endless energy are two of the four pillars of making the workplace work, and for the first time, we need to squarely face our fears and insecurities to move forward. It's time to tap into our courage and address the ABCs of workplace negativity: asshats, bullies, and complainers.

Before we jump in, I need to make sure that you are not one of the ABCs yourself.

Sorry, but we need to do this first. If you are not sure where you stand, ask one of the people in your Solutionist Society to make a candid assessment of your on-the-job behavior. Give three of your colleagues the "Are You Making Work Work? Quiz" (page 31) and ask them to *honestly* answer the questions with you in mind. Or simply take the time to evaluate how you are presenting yourself in the workplace before you move forward.

Why is this so important? Because, as I have said before, the same kind of thinking that created this mess is incapable of solving it. Just as more darkness cannot brighten up an already dark room, more rudeness and negativity cannot make a more positive workplace. If you are not mentally or emotionally ready to address the ABCs in a positive manner, you will make your situation worse, not better. Trust me on this.

Now that we have that out of the way, and you are convinced that you are ready, let's start by defining and dealing with the first of the three archenemies of *Making Work Work*.

Enter the Asshats.

ASSHATS, DEFINED

A few years ago, one of my good friends, named Heather, had her lunch stolen from the refrigerator at work. She had brought in leftover take-out food from her favorite restaurant and she was drooling over the idea of diving into it at lunchtime.

When she opened up the refrigerator, however, her lunch bag was half open, and her take-out food was gone. The unknown thief even took her plasticware! To say that Heather was furious was an understatement.

First, let me give you a little context. Heather is one of the nicest human beings on the face of the earth. In a little over three years that I have personally known her, I've never heard her utter a curse word once.

So you can imagine my shock when I heard her grab her empty lunch bag and angrily shake it above her head as she exclaimed, "Who's the asshat who stole my lunch?!"

Getting your lunch stolen is not funny at all, but seeing such a sweet woman lose her cool and yell out a made-up word was, well . . . pretty funny.

"Heather, did you just say 'asshat'?" I asked.

"Yes, I did! Anyone who would steal someone's lunch is definitely an asshat!" And then she stormed off in a homicidal rage in search of one very unlucky lunch bag bandit.

From that moment on, *asshat* has been one of my favorite words.

An asshat, as I later found out, is not a made-up word. It is defined as a person who has his head figuratively shoved up his butt and is utterly clueless about the world around him. Moreover, since his ass is now on his head, this person is known as an asshat. Even worse, with their heads up their asses, asshats are usually selfish, rude, and inconsiderate because they are unable to see anything outside of themselves.

I'm sure that this sounds a little more familiar now. While I do enjoy the word asshat, this isn't about calling people names (there's nothing positive about that). This is solely about identifying asshat-like behavior, and dealing with it productively. Do you work with anyone who acts like an asshat? If so, let's talk about how to keep him from derailing this movement.

DEALING WITH THE DARK ARTS OF ASSHATRY

In chapter 2, we discussed the dangers of incivility, which are basically the dark arts of asshatry in disguise. Here is the list (which isn't an exhaustive one, so feel free to add to it) again:

- Gossiping
- Lack of cell phone etiquette
- Belittling others' efforts
- Poor email etiquette: Sending an email without a greeting, using all caps, cc'ing the world on every email that she sends out

- Purposely failing to acknowledge a "Hello" or "Good morning"
- Ignoring employees' or coworkers' concerns, thoughts, or input
- Not cleaning up after yourself or expecting others to clean up your messes
- Stealing or "forgetting" to share credit for a job well done
- Flaking out on scheduled meetings, being consistently late, or purposely keeping people waiting
- Casting the blame on others for your own mistakes
- Constant moodiness
- Failing to say "Please," "Thank you," "I'm sorry," or "Excuse me."
- Coming into work sick and spreading your germs to others
- Eye rolling, loud sighing, head-shaking, etc., when someone is talking
- Interrupting constantly and not listening
- Withholding information
- Criticizing people in front of others
- Swiping through your cell phone or otherwise not paying attention during a meeting
- Being loud and/or inconsiderate of others working nearby

The lack of consideration and basic common courtesy can be infuriating.

Who raised these people? What type of knucklehead acts like this in a professional setting? I want to roundhouse kick these fools in their asshats.

It is easy to drift into a downward spiral of wanting to respond to rudeness with even more rudeness or to fight fire with fire, but we can't. Sorry. As Solutionists, we must repeatedly reject that extremely tempting and delicious-looking bait.

This eye-for-an-eye silliness is the type of thinking that created this problem in the first place. We cannot forget why we are doing this. Are we here to satisfy our momentary emotional impulses or are we here to transcend these issues and change the world?

One of the most powerful tools I use to keep myself sane when dealing with asshats is something I learned as a child. Even though I don't consider myself religious (I'm more of a spiritual type of guy), I receive a lot of peace from the very well-known Serenity Prayer:

> *God [feel free to insert "universe," "subconscious mind," or whatever you believe in], grant me the serenity to accept the things I cannot change, the courage to change the things I can, and the wisdom to know the difference.*

These are the only options that will ever make sense when dealing with difficult people.

1. The Serenity to Accept: Dealing with What Is

Your boss suffers from serious mood swings and manages his emotions like a sleep-deprived toddler.

Your colleague is always right (or more annoyingly, never wrong) and has an excuse for every one of her shortcomings.

Your company just changed the dress code, and now you have to wear a uniform that makes you want to angrily smash every mirror in sight.

You were just notified that there will be companywide pay cuts, effective immediately.

Do you know what all four of those situations have in common? *There is very little, if anything, that you can do to change them.*

I know, that isn't what you wanted to hear, but it's true. Think about it for a moment. Is there something that you can do right now to bolster your boss's emotional intelligence, fix your colleague's unwillingness to take personal ownership, reverse your company's new dress code, or alter the fact that your pay just got slashed?

If your answer is yes, then I highly recommend that you get to work and do what you need to do to improve your situation. If your answer is no, does it really make any sense to spend an ounce of your precious time and energy fighting against those things?

If you cannot change something, the only positive option is acceptance.

Read the last sentence again. How does that make you feel? Defeated? Pissed off? Ready to throw your hands in the air and give up? If so, that is probably because you don't have a useful definition of *acceptance*.

Contrary to popular belief, acceptance is not a passive activity. If your boss is known to have mood swings that fluctuate as wildly as American gas prices, instead of driving yourself crazy about her lack of emotional control and how she should be acting, you can acknowledge the reality of who she is and keep moving forward. Acceptance is not saying that you condone her behavior, understand her behavior, or even respect her behavior.

Acceptance, at its core, is telling the truth to yourself about the reality that is in front of you.

Sure, your boss and your coworker should grow up or see a therapist, and your company should have warned you about the dress code and the pay cut—*but it didn't happen.* As the iconic life strategist Tony Robbins would say, *Stop shoulding on yourself.* There are no amount of shoulds that will have the slightest effect on changing the reality of what is front of you. We are here to deal with what's real, and we cannot make the workplace work if we are unable to fully accept reality with complete clarity.

Acceptance is not about rolling over like a coward and dealing with life's beat downs with a masochistic resignation and a smile. Remember, right now we are solely talking about the things that you *cannot* change. Are you a coward if you choose to stop wishing that you could travel back in time and rewrite your entire work history? No, that is not cowardice—that is called preventing a nervous breakdown. Save your fight for what you can change.

If you don't think this is possible in your current workplace situation, consider this: Many prisoners of war understood this concept fully.

Throughout our country's history, captured soldiers during wartime spent years enduring unimaginable horrors. But instead of fighting and denying the reality that was in front of them, they focused their energy on what they could control. They were trapped in a savage hellhole where they would be tortured, starved, and dehumanized without any end in sight. Fighting against this brutal reality—*one that they could not change*—would only serve to accelerate their descent into madness.

So, instead, they clung onto the sliver of life that remained within their control. They offered emotional support to their fellow captive troops in any way possible, even if it was merely tapping on the wall to let the other prisoners know they were still with them. They walked laps in their impossibly small prison cells to keep in shape and to be physically ready to endure the inevitable torture that awaited them. They prayed and developed a deeper spiritual connection that helped them to soldier on for another day. Most importantly, they saved their fight for what they could change. I believe this sharpened focus helped save their lives.

Maybe it can save ours, too.

And make no mistake: Maneuvering around the unchangeable circumstances in our lives is a lifesaving skill.

I can say with confidence that I have positively changed and learned more from dealing with the difficult colleagues, bosses, and circumstances I could not change, than I ever did from the ideal ones. If you are like me, you have probably learned resilience, patience, resourcefulness, and courage in the process. And, as the quote at the beginning of this chapter alluded to, you have discovered exactly the person and leader you will never become. These gifts are hard-earned and should not be taken lightly.

We do not have to be able to change the circumstances in our lives to control their effect on us. Regardless of the unchangeable circumstances we're facing, the choice is ours to commit to living each step of the Attitude Adjustment Pyramid. We can strengthen our connection to our friends and our inner circle, we can silently laugh at the insanity of it all, or we can simply reframe the situation entirely.

Or we can fight with every ounce of our being against the circumstances that we can *change.*

If that's your choice, read on.

2. The Courage to Change: Being Assertive versus Being Aggressive

I do not believe that we can change other people.

I have been working in the people business for over a decade, and I have never succeeded in changing anyone. That would be an embarrassingly pathetic track record if changing people were my goal (thankfully, it's not). Changing the well-adjusted people in our lives is practically impossible, so what chance is there to change a person who behaves like an asshat on a daily basis? Less than zero. The truth is that people can only change themselves when they are ready to change.

Our job is to provide the information and the awareness to expedite that process.

This process will require some serious courage.

If you have to have a challenging, but necessary, conversation with a coworker or boss about something that has become intolerable for you, chances are you will be scared to do it. I get it—just know that your fear is okay and completely normal. Fear is going to accompany you on every step of this journey. You cannot make it go away, so you will have to do the next best thing: *Take action in spite of your fears.*

To me, that's courage. And one of the best ways to display that courage is to be assertive.

For some people, that may sound scary and worrisome, especially if you have a passive and nonconfrontational personality. If so, I'm right there with you. I'm a nonconfrontational guy. The good news is that assertiveness is a learned skill, and if I can learn it, anyone can.

Being assertive means that you are willing to consistently stand up for yourself in a positive and respectful way.

Aggressiveness, on the other hand, is all about getting your needs met by force, without any regard to how it impacts anyone else. As far as I'm concerned, assertiveness and aggressiveness are polar opposites. One is a crucial skill needed to create a positive work environment, while the other has the power to destroy healthy communication, teamwork, and this movement in a flash.

If a coworker is exhibiting an asshat behavior that is driving you crazy, and you believe that you can positively change the circumstances by calling her attention to it, then it is up to you to have the conversation with her—scared or not. It is entirely possible that she may not be aware of her asshat behavior and/or the effect it is having on you. Her head is figuratively up her own butt, after all.

Remember the L.I.N.E. strategy from chapter 6? This is different. The L.I.N.E. strategy is in response to someone violating the boundary that you placed around your priorities. Assertively bringing awareness to asshat behavior, on the other hand, does not have to be due to a violation of your boundaries. It is about addressing any behavior that you feel is unacceptable and that you want to stop. Because of this, it requires a different, but equally straightforward strategy.

1. Respectfully and clearly state the facts of the problem.
2. Ask the person to take action to solve the problem.

Here are a few common workplace examples of inconsiderate asshat behavior and three ways to deal with it. As you will see, one of these styles is not like the others in terms of its potential effectiveness and its ability to create positive change.

Example #1:

Your coworkers consistently leave the break room a mess.

Aggressive: "Enough is enough! I'm tired of feeling as if I'm working in a damn college dorm room! Were you raised by animals? Clean up after yourselves, you filthy slobs!"

Asshat: Pile the empty cups and dirty plates in their cubicles with a note that says, "Hey, I think you forgot this."

Assertive: "Hey, guys. Your trash has been on the tables in the break room since early this morning and it is starting to smell bad in there. Can you please clean up your mess before it gets worse?"

Example #2:

A coworker forgets (or chooses not) to share credit on a successful project.

Aggressive: "Did you seriously submit our project without listing me as a contributor? What in hell is wrong with you? Do you think I'm too stupid to notice what you did?"

Asshat <twists mustache in villainous fashion>: That's cool. He can enjoy his time in the sun for now. Next time he asks me for help,

I'm going to completely sabotage the project and watch him crash and burn in epic fashion. That will show him.

Assertive: "Hey, Mike. I'm concerned that I wasn't mentioned as a contributor to this project. I worked very hard on it and I was hoping that my contributions would be recognized and appreciated. Can you tell me what happened?"

Example #3:

A coworker engages in loud and personal cell phone conversations nearby while you are trying to work.

Aggressive: "Seriously? SHUT UP! People are trying to work here! No one wants to hear about the drama that you're having with your husband. He probably doesn't love you anyway. Shut your mouth and get to work!"

Asshat: Accidentally spill your coffee on her cell phone when she's not looking. Oopsie!

Assertive: "Carrie, I'm really struggling to concentrate. Do you mind keeping it down a little bit or taking the conversation outside?"

Example #4:

A coworker criticizes you and/or your work in front of other colleagues or customers.

Aggressive: "I'm sick and tired of you trying to one-up me in front of other people. I swear, if you do it again, you're going to have a real problem on your hands!"

Asshat: Make up false rumors about your coworker so that his credibility will be irreparably damaged the next time he tries to speak to anyone about anything.

Assertive <pull your coworker aside privately>: "Keith, I feel that it damages my credibility when you expose my shortcomings and correct me in front of others. If there is something that you feel the need to correct, I would appreciate if you would do it privately. Can we agree to this going forward?"

You get the point. Once you have made the decision to facilitate the process of pulling someone's head out of his ass by raising his awareness, this simple two-step assertive communication model will help you in virtually any situation. As you already guessed, aggressiveness or, worse, being an asshat will accomplish nothing.

Does this work on bosses, too? Of course. With a boss, it helps to err on the softer side of assertiveness. For example:

Boss Example #1:

He is overloading you with work.

Assertive response: "Right now I'm working on four things that all seem to be equally important. Which project would you like me to concentrate on first?"

Boss Example #2:

She communicates unclearly and expects you to read her mind to determine what she is asking you to do.

Assertive response: "I want to be sure that I meet your expectations. This is what I gathered from your meeting [or email] (summarize it in bullets). Before I begin, is this correct?"

Boss Example #3:

He swipes through his cell phone during your one-on-one meetings while you're talking.

Assertive response <Pause until he stops looking at his phone and gives you his attention>: "You looked busy, and I didn't want to interrupt. Is it okay for me to continue?"

Does this sound hard to you? That's because *it is* hard, at first! Just like riding a bicycle, swimming, developing a meditation practice, or playing a musical instrument, it requires practice to master the art of assertive communication. Everything is hard before it is easy.

The real question is this: Are you willing to fight through your fears to overcome this challenge?

Excellent, because it is about to get a lot harder.

THE WORST OF ALL ASSHAT BEHAVIORS: PASSIVE-AGGRESSIVENESS

Passive-aggressiveness is the grand master of all asshat behaviors, and, as I'm sure you already know, it is very difficult to deal with. It's one of the most challenging personality types to deal with in any social or professional interaction.

Passive-aggressiveness is the inability, or unwillingness, to express hostility or anger directly. It also gives offenders the added benefit of not having to own it when they are called out on it.

You are familiar with passive-aggressive people's go-to bag of tricks, I'm sure. Constant sulking, undermining and/or sabotaging projects that they're not interested in, deliberately failing to respond to emails, mumbling under their breath as they are walking away, backhanded compliments, biting sarcasm, cc'ing the entire universe on emails unnecessarily . . . the list goes on and on.

This is worth mentioning again, because it is easy to forget this key point: *The workplace positivity movement isn't about changing passive-aggressive people, or anyone else.* And that's a good thing because changing a passive-aggressive person is as close to an impossibility as there is.

One of the key ways to dealing with passive-aggressive people is not to give them what they want.

Passive-aggressive people are trying to covertly express their anger. Because they are angry, some of these people want to hurt you in some way. When you react by showing pain, that gives them the fuel to continue to hurt you. Strange and twisted, I know. We are not here to play armchair psychologist and figure out why they are angry, we just need to limit the effect of their suppressed anger on us. *The solution is never to take the bait.* For example:

Example #1:
The backhanded compliment

"Nice presentation, that was so much better than the one you gave last week."

Desired reaction: "What was wrong with last week's presentation?!" or "Wow, that was rude. Why do you have to be like that?"

Better reaction <said with sincerity, not sarcasm>: "I really appreciate that, thanks! I'm working hard to get better each day, and I'm glad you noticed."

Example #2:
Sulking or pouting (for any reason)

You: "Hey, Sandy. Is everything cool?"

Sandy <clearly upset about something>: "I'm fine."

You: "You sure? You seem upset about something."

Sandy: "I said, I'm fine."

You: "Okay, I'm glad to hear that!" Then keep acting like all is fine, and take her at her word.

Example #3:
Biting Sarcasm

Asshat <as you enter the room>: "Hey everyone, look who just showed up for the meeting! Someone better turn on the air-conditioning because the hot air is going to start flowing now!"

You <said with curiosity and confusion>: "I don't get it."

There is a great deal of power in the "I don't get it" response. Responding with a flat "I don't get it" after someone's lame attempt at passive-aggressive humor (such as a racist joke) and, better yet, having the person try to explain his pitiful attempt at humor are excellent ways to shut down the situation in a hurry.

Or, if the passive-aggressive person is extremely persistent, feel free to address her behavior directly, using the two-step assertive communication strategy presented earlier in this chapter. The key is to respond to passive-aggressiveness without ever getting emotional. Why? *Because it is exhausting for passive-aggressive people to do something over and over again and not get the results they want.*

Passive-aggressive asshats find their bliss by manipulating your emotions like a master puppeteer. That's why the worst thing that you can do is lose your cool and get upset, because they can easily hide behind their veiled anger and innocently say, "What's the big deal? I was just trying to be funny. Lighten up and stop being so sensitive."

And then, guess who ends up looking like the jerk? You guessed it—you. You can't let that happen.

Regardless of the situation, if you have decided to tap into your courage in hopes of positively changing the situation, don't half-step—put all your energy into doing it. Use assertive communication, refuse to take the passive-aggressive person's bait, or limit your interactions with her. Instead, do what is necessary to address this behavior and don't let it get in the way of positively improving your career and your workplace.

The Wisdom to Know the Difference: Getting Off the Fence

So here we are on the fence and a decision needs to be made. What are you going to do?

Accept your circumstances or change them? Find your serenity or find your courage?

Only you can answer these deeply personal questions as you deal with the asshats in your life. Each day you ignore this choice is another day when you declare to the world that you are not ready to move forward. That fate is not for you. *I believe you are ready.* You wouldn't be reading these words right now if you weren't.

So act like it.

Jump.

But what if you jump to the wrong side and mistakenly choose acceptance over assertiveness, or vice versa? That will happen—count on it. We are not here to get everything right on the first try. Our job is to pivot, course-correct, make adjustments, change plans. Call it what you want, but it all boils down to acting in spite of our fears and fixing our mistakes along the way. This is how we will keep the movement going forward.

This is the only path to becoming wise enough to know the difference—there are no shortcuts to gaining this wisdom. Action will be your guide and experience will be your teacher when you are ready to decide.

Are you ready, Solutionist?

R.E.A.L. WORK
Assignment #7:

The Courage to Change

Dealing with asshatlike behavior at work is rarely an enjoyable process, but we can still take action to ensure that the process is as painless and successful as possible. The first step is to determine which less-than-ideal situations you should accept (write them down on the left side of a blank page), and which ones you should take action to change (write them down on the right side of a blank page.). For the purposes of this assignment, our focus will be on the situations that you believe could positively change by calling attention to the other person's behavior.

For this assignment, choose one challenging situation that you are having with a person who is behaving like an asshat and have an assertive conversation with her about it. Wait, there's more. You only have *one week* from reading this assignment to doing it. This conversation will not get any easier by procrastinating indefinitely, so I'm putting a time limit on this. Seven days. Understand that the fear you are feeling right now isn't going anywhere, so you are going to have to act in spite of it. If you have determined that a situation has become intolerable for you, follow the two-step assertive communication strategy outlined in this chapter.

When you have finished, write down the answer to these two questions: (1) How did it go? And (2) How do you feel now that it's over? Oftentimes, you'll be shocked at the positive outcomes you will experience afterward.

CHAPTER

11

DEALING WITH THE ABCs OF WORKPLACE NEGATIVITY

ABC #2: Bullies

There is overwhelming evidence that the higher the level of self-esteem, the more likely one will be to treat others with respect, kindness and generosity.

—NATHANIEL BRANDEN

I want to step aside and introduce you to Whitney—a brilliant and strong-willed woman who exemplifies resilience. She was one of the many people I interviewed for this book, and I believe that her story will resonate with millions of people around the world.

Here is her story in her own words:

It's truly frightening how powerfully that one person can affect us. One toxic person, even when encountered just once a day, can poison your mood, happiness, and even your self-respect. I've always loved Eleanor Roosevelt's saying: "No one can make you feel inferior without your consent," but this isn't always easily done.

I worked for a couple of years with a woman named Alice who ran a department that my job required me to collaborate with on a daily basis. Before meeting her on my first day with the company, it was made crystal clear by other colleagues that Alice was a "strong-willed individual who ran a tight ship." What I wasn't warned about was the fact that she was a full-blown, grown-up, schoolyard bully who took delight and pleasure in publicly belittling and humiliating her colleagues. I was never clear on whether it was for entertainment or to reinforce her sense of power, but I suspect it was a twisted combination of both.

Alice was a calculating, manipulative, cruel woman. She played people against one another, watching them with glee as they ripped each other (and themselves) apart. She was also incredibly intelligent, so while she was often called on her behavior by senior management (and had a file in Human Resources so thick it wouldn't fit in a single drawer), she somehow had them wrapped around her finger and managed to wriggle her way out of just about anything. Many people spoke openly about how, over her eighteen years with the company, she had acquired so much knowledge and dirt on senior management that she was able to blackmail her way out of anything. I often wondered how much truth there was to that story.

The unfortunate thing about Alice, and bullies in general, really, is that she almost always saved her bullying for moments when she had an audience in an effort to inspire fear and establish a sense of authority. For whatever reason, she had it in for me from early on. When I was scheduled to work in her department with members of her team, she would storm in, point her finger at me, and yell, "What are you doing here? You are no use to us and have no reason to be here. Get out. You are dismissed!" Dismissed? It was as if she were an angry schoolteacher scolding a young child who was caught trespassing in an area where she wasn't supposed to be. There was one occasion when I was speaking to her while several of her employees were there and she held her hand up to me and yelled, "Just shut up!" For the first time, I walked right up to her and simply said, "Nobody speaks to me that way, Alice. Not even you." For a week thereafter, members of her team approached me carefully to quietly thank me for standing up to her.

Over the years I sought help to address this situation in just about every way I could. When our company distributed confidential surveys to provide employees with an opportunity to give open feedback regarding our colleagues and our work environment, I cited examples of the consistent abuse and lack of respect that Alice demonstrated. When that didn't change anything, I went to Human Resources, who repeatedly promised they would speak with her, but nothing ever came of it. I then approached her boss, and when that didn't help I met with her boss's boss. Sadly, nothing ever changed, and Alice was never held accountable for her words or her actions. While this was infuriating, it taught me a valuable life lesson: When a company (or a person) allows a bully to get away with abusive behavior, they are openly validating such behavior while actively demonstrating a gross lack of concern for the hundreds of people who are potentially affected by that individual. In unfortunate circumstances such as these, it's up to us to take care of ourselves. In my case, I resigned . . . and it was the healthiest decision I could have made to take care of myself.

Thanks for sharing that story, Whitney. Her story exemplifies the unfiltered ugliness that is known as workplace bullying. It destroys self-esteem, it destroys careers, and it even destroys lives. And, as you are reading these words, this epidemic is spreading through America and the world like a life-threatening plague. As Whitney found out the hard way, being on the wrong end of workplace bullying is not a problem that is easily solved. She completed confidential surveys, she went to Human Resources, she went to her boss's boss, and she even confronted the bully directly. Nothing worked.

So how can we keep the movement going strong when dealing with the near-invincible supervillain known as the workplace bully?

If you have ever read comic books, you know that every villain has a weakness. We just have to tap into our patience, creativity, and resilience to find it.

The process begins by truly understanding what we're up against.

THE TRUTH ABOUT WORKPLACE BULLYING

I have talked to thousands of people about the horrors of workplace bullying. I have found that, after reading Whitney's story, most people would usually fall into one of three camps:

1. They fully understand the dangers of workplace bullying, and not only would they never engage in that type of behavior, but they are also committed to doing anything in their power to make it stop.
2. They say that they fall into the first category, but they lack the emotional intelligence and/or self-awareness to realize that they consistently engage in the bullying behaviors they claim to despise.
3. They roll their eyes at the term *workplace bullying* and consider it an annoying buzzword or, even worse, a convenient excuse used by lazy employees who have a personality conflict at work or who are being held accountable for not doing their work properly.

Don't be on the wrong side of history.

Workplace bullying is not a make-believe issue that only affects tenderhearted employees unfit to deal with the challenges of surviving in the hard-nosed world of business. This is a life-destroying epidemic that is negatively affecting the lives of millions of people all over the globe. Companies on every continent are currently losing billions of dollars each year as a result of workplace bullying, which leads to loss of productivity, miscommunication, lack of motivation, rampant employee turnover, lawsuits, and increased health-care costs.

Speaking of health, millions of employees facing workplace bullying are dealing with life-altering issues, such as hypertension, sleeplessness, ulcers, panic attacks, migraine headaches, clinical depression, and addictions like alcoholism or drug abuse. In extreme cases, workplace bullying can even result in suicide.

The global economy is suffering enormously from workplace bullying and, on an individual basis, it is eroding health, ripping apart families, and lowering quality of life. It is safe to say that anyone who is contributing to this problem in any way is actively making the world a worse place for all of us.

Let's begin by clearly defining what this problem is so that we can deal with it effectively. There are a lot of definitions of workplace bullying, but here is the one that I believe is the best:

> ***Repeated, unreasonable actions of individuals (or a group) directed toward an employee (or a group of employees), which are intended to intimidate, degrade, humiliate, or undermine; or which create a risk to the health or safety of the employee(s).***[1]

For the people in group 3, mentioned earlier, let's be clear about something: *Being held accountable for doing our jobs properly does not constitute workplace bullying.* Bullying has nothing to do with receiving a poor performance evaluation or negative feedback about a failed project. Employees are not running to their Human Resources Departments in droves because they didn't receive a proper greeting from their bosses in the morning. Lawyers all over the world are not lying in wait for an employee to be on the wrong end of a verbal outburst at work, so they can chalk up another case in the win column.

If you are reading this and believe that 65 million Americans (and millions more all over the globe) are reporting these events as workplace bullying, you are either deluded or grasping at excuses to continue using other people as your emotional punching bags. Either way, let me say something directly to you that your bullying victims can't say: You are a societal menace and unfit to be working with the rest of us. The same goes for the fringe employees who may be reporting these events as workplace bullying.

As we already noted, workplace bullying consists of repeated and unreasonable actions. This is by no means an exhaustive list, but here are some examples of bullying behavior in the workplace:

- Sabotaging your work and/or purposely giving you incorrect information
- Verbal abuse (excessive cursing, yelling, name-calling, condescension)
- Humiliating and/or embarrassing an employee privately or, even worse, publicly
- Purposefully excluding and isolating you from the rest of the team
- Making baseless accusations against you
- Overloading you with work and/or establishing impossible deadlines that are setting you up to fail
- Taking away all your work to engender a feeling of uselessness
- Spreading false rumors and gossiping about you
- Dumping the least desirable assignments or work schedules on you
- Hurling insults and constantly lashing out at you with destructive criticism (constructive criticism is always fine)
- Withholding critical information and/or resources you need to do your job
- Constantly changing work expectations and expecting you to read the bully's mind
- Making threats and using intimidation, either verbally or nonverbally (such as gestures or glaring)

I am confident that most people, even those in group 3, would agree that any of these behaviors, if done repeatedly, would contribute to a hostile work environment. Every person, department, and organization engaging in this behavior or, worse, condoning this kind of behavior in the name of productivity, will fail. The best talent will leave, potential talent will stay away, and the employees who are left behind to work in a bullying environment will only do the minimum to keep from being fired.

This is not a recipe for success, and that is what the bully fails to realize. Whatever benefits accrue from condoning this type of behavior are always temporary and unsustainable.

FEAR ALWAYS FAILS

This is not a philosophical discussion. Fear is a lazy, primitive, and completely ineffective way to lead. And, as a motivational tool, it will always fail. Always. It may temporarily gain you people's bodies, but it is incapable of winning their hearts. And it is people's hearts that will change the world.

So why do so many people resort to fear as their go-to motivational tactic, if all it does is break down meaningful communication and stifle the sharing of ideas and innovation while undermining teamwork and camaraderie, creating mistrust, diminishing productivity, and costing organizations all over the world untold millions of dollars? Especially when there are far better tools available, like kindness, respect, and positivity?

The answer is that the bullies are scared, too. More than you will ever be.

No, I'm not looking to generate sympathy for the bullies who are making your life a living hell. I couldn't care less about why they are scared, and you shouldn't, either. This is solely about understanding what makes these people tick.

At their core, bullies are cowards. The appearance of toughness and power is nothing more than a desperate attempt to mask the fear and inner brokenness that torments them on a daily basis. But don't be fooled by their tough guy/tough gal, smoke-and-mirrors routine for a moment longer.

Because bullies are so scared, they seek power and control as cure-all drugs to make the fear go away. Even stranger, once they see that people are scared of them, that makes them feel more powerful, which makes the fear subside temporarily. But the fear never goes away. So they keep searching for new targets to intimidate and control, like a junkie fumbling around in dark alleys and seedy dive bars for his next fix.

In the end, they need your fear to survive. Without your

fear, they are nothing. Your fear is their fix. Your pain is their power.

Sadly, bullies rarely change. In many cases, using fear as a tool was a strategy they learned as kids on the playground. The bullies who ripped off my favorite jacket and peed on it in junior high school are forty-year-old adults now. They may share a cubicle wall with you or, worse, be the boss.

Bullies are not very skilled. Sure, they may be cunning and manipulative, but, in reality, they are like a carpenter whose only tool is a hammer. Unfortunately, if that's the only tool in their tool kit, then it doesn't take long for them to see everything in their path as a nail.

Let's talk about how to avoid getting hit.

DEALING WITH WORKPLACE BULLIES

I always cringe when I read articles with headlines like this: "The Surefire Way to Deal with Bullying." When it comes to human behavior, there is no surefire way to do anything. The only surefire thing about dealing with bullies in the workplace is that you are definitely going to need some help, beginning with the help that you must give yourself.

Step 1: Call It What It Is

Take another look at the bulleted list of bullying behaviors on page 149. Are you repeatedly on the receiving end of those kinds of behaviors? If so, then make today the day you stop rationalizing and minimizing what is happening to you. You are not weak-minded. You are not incapable of dealing with the challenges of the real world of work. You don't need to develop a thicker skin.

You are being bullied at work. Stop calling it anything but what it is.

This is not a small step. It is the most important part of effectively dealing with workplace bullying. As soon as you make it clear to yourself that you are being bullied, you can make the life-affirming decision to do something about it. You won't take any action without first making a decision, and you won't make a decision until you face up to the abuse you're receiving.

Step 2: Get Help from Your Buddies

There is always power in numbers, especially when it comes to bullying. In chapter 8, I discussed the countless reasons you need to have friends at work, and this is another extremely important reason: *They can support you against the bully.*

Bullies often target more than one person in an attempt to exert even more control. As far as the bully is concerned, having a group of people she can control is better than having just one person under her thumb. If that is the case in your workplace, use this to your advantage.

To effectively deal with workplace bullying, your most potent weapon will be the believability of your case. Your believability increases with the number of people who are willing to support you in your complaint, as long as it's done correctly (more on this in step 4). The key is identifying someone you trust who has your back and is fully with you in your quest to make the bullying stop. That is why you should get this person on your side beforehand. It could be disastrous to share your plans with someone who may run back to the bully in an attempt to win favor with her.

This step is not a requirement, but it will definitely make things a little easier. If you feel as if you are the only one being targeted or there is no one you can trust, then it's time to turn to the next step.

Step 3: Document Everything

Good documentation is an extremely powerful tool, and one whose value cannot be overstated.

If you're dealing with a boss or a colleague who is known for his bullying, you need to tap into your inner investigative newspaper reporter and stealthily record every instance of bullying against you. One of the things that many bullying bosses count on is the lack of a quality paper trail put together by the people they bully.

Keep track of everything relating to the bullying incidents, including exact quotes (if possible), dates, times, who was present, where it happened—everything. If your bullying boss is dumb enough to bolster your case by bullying you in writing or otherwise (emails, text messages, voice-mail messages, and the like), then he's basically doing your documentation work for you. Just smile, and keep every single shred of it—and back it up.

Keep in mind that when you're documenting the bullying perpetrated against you, stick to the facts, not your emotions. This is not a journaling exercise for you to do a deep dive into how the bully's behavior reminds you of how your parents used to talk to you as a child. This is about collecting credible evidence. You shouldn't spend a moment of your time documenting your feelings. That's the quickest way to demolish your case. Dealing with a workplace bully isn't easy, and if you want the bullying to stop, you're going to have to stick to the facts.

Use a note-taking app on your phone or, if you're an old-school type, keep a notepad and pen with you constantly. Whatever you do, don't rely on your memory. If you have a coworker you trust implicitly, someone who feels the same way about the bully as you do, have her document her experiences, too. There's strength in numbers and there's strength in consistency, too.

A consistent pattern of multiple incidents of bullying behavior cannot be easily explained away, especially if this behavior is clearly creating a hostile work environment for you and others. Your documentation is the Holy Grail that clearly shows the intent behind the behavior. And if your documentation reveals a pattern of intentionally vicious behavior, the organization really has no choice but to take action.

Step 4: State Your Business Case

In speaking with countless bullied employees throughout my career and on my blog, there is the one common, disillusioning thread that ties many of these people together: They do not believe that their Human Resources (HR) Departments are there to help and protect them from harm. Generally speaking, I can see their point—even the most elite Human Resources Departments in America often struggle when it comes to adequately serving workplace bullying victims. If you disagree with this or think that Human Resources Departments as a whole are successfully dealing with the workplace bullying epidemic plaguing our country, just ask a workplace bullying victim. You will be surprised by what you will find. Or not.

Many Human Resources Departments all over the world are filled with an army of risk managers who are trying to save the company from financial loss, lawsuits, and bad press. That is why it doesn't make any sense to approach an HR representative with stories about how much you don't like the bully, how the bullying is affecting your ability to be a fully present parent to your two young children, or how your acid reflux is starting to flare up again due to the stress of being bullied.

All day long HR representatives hear sob stories from employees who are being bullied, and many Human Resources staffers are understandably desensitized to it. They care about keeping their own jobs, and as mentioned earlier, their jobs are to protect the company. Worse, many of them are burned out from being an emotional dumping ground for problems they are often helpless to solve.

Instead, you need to start thinking like an HR representative. In order for your complaint to stand out in a sea of highly emotional complaints, you need to present a legitimate business case to make it easier for the HR representative to help you.

First, do your homework. Does your organization have an antibullying policy? If so, make sure you clearly show in your documentation how the bully's behavior violates that policy.

Next, specify how the bullying behavior is affecting the business's bottom line. Let's use turnover as an example. If seven people left your department in the past year, how much would that cost? The Workplace Bullying Institute came up with an excellent formula.[2] The cost of all turnover-related activities (recruitment, training, lost productivity, etc.) is estimated by multiplying the combined salaries of the people who quit by 1.5, which is a conservative estimate.

Using this example, seven employees, making $50,000 a year each, amounts to $350,000 a year. If you multiply $350,000 by 1.5, that equals $525,000 a year. So unchecked bullying cost this department over a half a million dollars this year in turnover-related expenses. Anyone with a shred of financial sense would have a very hard time excusing the loss of that kind of money—especially when it is due to something that is preventable.

If you don't have turnover numbers, you're going to have to get creative. How has the bullying affected absenteeism? Do your best to calculate hourly salaries against time away from the office (for instance, $20/hour x 15 hours out sick). If you have employee engagement survey information or customer satisfaction information available that will support your argument, include that in your report. If the bullying is real, you can definitely create a case against it.

TO STAND UP OR NOT TO STAND UP?

I want you to think about something.

When workplace bullying is reported, employers ignore the bullying in 44 percent of cases. In 18 percent of cases, they take the side of the bully and worsen the situation.[3]

Those statistics aren't overwhelmingly positive and in many cases that is enough to stop people from taking action and to keep them living in silent misery. Here is my take on this: We must take action for necessary change to happen.

> We must take sides. Neutrality helps the oppressor, never the victim. Silence encourages the tormentor, never the tormented.
>
> —ELIE WIESEL

Even worse, you may work for a small company that doesn't have a Human Resources Department or any centralized resource to go to for assistance. In that case, your choices are limited to only two options: (1) Assertively address the bully using the skills outlined in the previous chapter, or (2) leave the company.

Acceptance is not an option that I ever recommend when it comes to workplace bullying. Unless you are locked away in a prison camp or you are enslaved, you should never accept a life of abuse as the way things have to be.

You're not on this earth to endure your work life and scratch off days on a cement wall like a prisoner awaiting the end of your sentence. If so, what will be your reward at retirement? A family you weren't able to fully engage with because you were too consumed with the bullying at work? Chronic health issues? Mental and emotional scars from years of abuse that you'll attempt to cover up with antidepressants, booze, and tears until you pitifully come to your merciful end in a pine box in the ground?

Screw that. Silence solves nothing.

This is about creating a movement in which kindness and mutual respect are the norms in every workplace, starting in yours. This is about making history, and until enough people speak out about the horrors of workplace bullying and the pain that it is causing millions of people, nothing will change. *Nothing.* Are you okay with that? I'm not. The new narrative starts today, and we're the ones holding the pen this time. I am committed to ending workplace bullying while I am alive, and I hope you will stand with me.

Is there a risk? Yes. Could we fail? Yes. Are these the wrong questions to ask? *Yes.*

I want you to think about what your life would be like if you choose to do nothing. What happens if you let fear win? How will that affect you? Your health? Your career? Your loved ones? Your sanity?

That's what scares me. The real risk is in doing nothing.

R.E.A.L. WORK

Assignment #8:

Creating the Case

Deciding to take positive action against a workplace bully is a terrifying endeavor, and if you have decided that you are willing to go down this road, you must have all your ducks in a row. For this assignment, the goal is to create the best business case you can. After you have determined that you are indeed being bullied at work, it's time to proceed.

1. Reach out to trusted members of your Solutionist Society. Are they dealing with the same treatment from the bully? Are they willing to stand with you? As with most things, there is strength in numbers.
2. Document everything. Keep track of every piece of information that will support your case—incriminating statements, emails, voice mails, everything. Leave your emotions out of it and stick to the facts.
3. Build your business case. If your company has an antibullying policy, use it to show how the bully's behavior directly violates it. Specify how the bully's actions are costing the company a great deal of money and that it is too costly to keep her around. The more meaningful information you can gather, the better.

The reality is that there is a risk in doing this. There is also a huge risk in doing nothing. It's up to you to decide which risk you are willing to live with.

CHAPTER

12

DEALING WITH THE ABCs OF WORKPLACE NEGATIVITY

ABC #3: Complainers

There are two types of people in this world, baby. The ones who make you feel good as soon as they walk into a room and the ones who make you feel good as soon as they walk out of it.

—LAURA RICHARDS (MY MOM)

Let's not mince words. Complaining is useless. That is why its debilitating toxicity has no place in this movement.

Before we get into how to immunize ourselves from the chronic complainers who are sapping our energy, we must first ensure that we are not engaging in this habit ourselves.

We can't complain our way into changing our lives, our workplaces, or the world. As Jeff Bezos, the founder of Amazon.com, once said, complaining is not a strategy. It is toxic and can pervert and twist this movement into a whiny support group of people who are stuck bitching about how much they hate their jobs while doing nothing to make their work lives better.

But we already know this, don't we? So why do we do it so often?

Because it is seductive, reaffirming, and, sometimes, it's even fun. It's nice to have our drama validated by others and to know that other people feel our pain. Even worse, because there seems to be a positive payoff when we do this (connection with others), complaining can be wildly addictive. And once you're hooked, you'll fool yourself into thinking that complaining is a worthwhile activity because it gives you a temporarily good feeling. But, then again, so does eating bacon-covered doughnuts, watching bad reality TV, or shooting heroin.

This movement is not about chasing a temporary high; it's about positively and permanently changing our work lives.

Complaining is damaging to the movement because it doesn't do anything to address the problem that we're facing. If anything, by complaining about the problem, we're now compounding the problem. Not only does the original problem still exist, but also by engaging in complaining, we're now less equipped to handle it.

VENTING VERSUS COMPLAINING

Many people confuse venting with complaining, so let me set the record straight.

Venting is a good thing. There is nothing helpful, healthy, or positive about bottling up your emotions and plastering a cheesy grin on your face because you don't want to appear negative to others. That is a recipe for an epic nervous breakdown that people will be talking about for years. Venting, on the other hand, will save your life.

Everyone needs to blow off steam for one reason or another, and that's what venting is all about. You might need to vent after you get off the phone with a ridiculously rude customer who is acting like a sailor with a toothache or after your bullying boss is doing her best *Devil Wears Prada* impression at your expense. It's cathartic.

Venting is a positive and healthy activity because there's a clear goal involved: You are appropriately releasing your negative feelings (anger, frustration, annoyance, and the like) about the situation and once you're done, you let it go. Done correctly, venting should be an intentional and temporary action. You can go to the gym for a tough workout, have a good cry, write an emotional letter then throw it away, share your frustrations with a trusted friend, or even punch a pillow repeatedly. This is not about wallowing in the situation for weeks, days, or even hours. You vent about the customer, your boss, the weather, or whatever, and then once it's off your chest, you put it in the rearview mirror and move on.

Complaining, on the other hand, may look similar to venting, but they are nothing alike. You have no clear goal when you're complaining. Complaining, unlike venting, isn't a temporary act of blowing off steam. Complaining is all about choosing to stay in a negative state for an indefinite period while projecting that negativity onto someone else. More often than not, complainers aren't even interested in finding a solution to what they're whining about. Complainers will whine and moan without listening to a word you have to say, and they'll happily take up as much of your time as you're willing to give them. Worst of all, if you allow them to, they'll end up dragging you down into their emotional cesspool with them.

Complainers also seem to be out of touch with the rest of the world and feel that they are the only ones dealing with drama. They often complain about the stuff that the rest of us also experience on a daily basis (long lines, bad weather, slow service at the restaurant, traffic, or rude people) as if it's somehow worse for them than it is for the rest of us. In addition, when they choose to complain about people, they tend to do it backward (they complain about work to their loved ones and they complain about their loved ones to their coworkers.)

A good way to recognize that you're venting and not complaining is that you should feel much better once you're done. Unlike venting, those engaged in complaining don't feel better after a marathon complaining session. If you don't believe me, just ask them.

Understanding the difference is a critical skill needed to actively contribute to this movement.

HOW TO KICK THE COMPLAINING HABIT COLD TURKEY

Chronic complaining is so devastating to this movement because it undermines our ability to creatively problem-solve the issue—and, as Solutionists, problem-solving is the name of this game. Instead of transcending the problem, we're handcuffing ourselves to it. We're allowing the asshats and the bullies of the working world to gain strength, while the movement fades away with a whimper. We can't talk away or think away our problems. Only action makes them go away.

Even the most well-intentioned Solutionist can fool himself into thinking that he's just venting when, in reality, he's chronically complaining. I know this because I myself suffered from that common delusion. The truth was that I wasn't venting, because it was far from a temporary, once-in-a-while type of a deal for me. I was stuck in a constant state of negativity, whining, and complaining.

As soon as something went wrong at work with one of my former bosses, I didn't even entertain the idea that there could be a nugget of positivity hidden inside the difficult situation. Instead, my brain merely cued up a ready-made complaint to dump on any sucker who was willing to listen.

> *"Why does she always have to publicly humiliate me in front of others?"*
>
> *"She yells at me like I'm one of her pet dogs who peed on her Coach purse. I'm sick and tired of her and her crap."*
>
> *"This woman has absolutely zero social skills. Was she raised by wolves or something?"*
>
> *"She would choke her own mother if it would get her promoted. She is soulless. I'll bet if a surgeon cut her open, she wouldn't even bleed—just a cloud of black smoke and flock of bats would come flying out."*

All those things were true, mind you (I still think the last one is true, too). It would have been fine if I had just vented and let it go, but I never did. The problem was that I would spend hours replaying the latest drama about her to anyone who would listen. There was nothing productive about my behavior because I had no interest in coming up with a solution, taking action, or even feeling better about the situation. I just whined and hoped that people would feel sorry for me and how hard my life was.

Thankfully, one of my friends, who was clearly sick and tired of my constant whining, challenged me to do something that was unthinkable to me at the time. He challenged me to go twenty-four hours without complaining about anything. At first I was a little annoyed, saying, "I'm not a complainer! I should be allowed to vent when I'm frustrated!" He didn't buy it and told me to humor him and try it—so I did.

The next twenty-four hours changed my life forever.

For the first time, I learned what it meant to truly live from conscious intention instead of unconsciously from habit. Whenever something happened to me that day that was less than ideal, I paused to notice the automatic complaint I was about to utter. And then something very simple, but incredibly powerful, happened next. I chose to think a different thought, and equally as important, I chose to say more empowering words instead. It sounds so simple, but I realized on that day, for the first time in my life, that I didn't have to be negative when faced with less-than-ideal circumstances. I could do something so much more useful:

I could focus on a solution instead.

This simple wisdom saved my relationships, saved my career, and, without a doubt, saved me from living a life that would be far from my best life. Whenever I feel myself drifting back into a complaining mode, I quickly do a twenty-four-hour complaining detox.

This includes, but is not limited to, refusing to complain about your job, your boss, your coworkers, your kids, your in-laws, your significant other (or lack of one), your finances, your health, your weight, the government, the weather, the traffic, how tired you are, how unappreciated you are, the fact that your favorite sports team can't seem to get it together, how you look in your pants, how much stuff you need to do this weekend, how hard it is to give up complaining (see what I did there?), and anything else you might be inclined to complain about.

It might be hard, but, then again, it's supposed to be hard. This isn't about hitting home runs, quick wins, or easy answers. This is about doing whatever it takes to make us better prepared to resolve our workplace drama. Even if it's hard.

Equally as important, when I choose to vent, I make a point of doing it intentionally and with the goal of finding a solution.

DEALING WITH COMPLAINERS

If you're confident that you have your complaining under control, sadly that's only half the battle. The other, and slightly trickier, half is to immunize yourself from the complainers who will happily drain you of your drive and stamina, if you let it happen. Here are three ways to protect yourself.

Step 1: Avoid the Secondhand Smoke

Years ago, I heard this analogy, and it accurately describes how I feel about chronic complainers. I don't smoke, and because of that I do everything that I can to limit my time around people who are smoking. I have dear friends who are smokers, but when they choose to light up, that's my cue to go. Why? Because I am not going to place myself in an environment for an extended period that will negatively affect my health. I have nothing against these friends who are smokers—I still love them as people—but I have to look out for myself.

I view chronic complaining in the same way.

If I am around someone who feels victimized on a daily basis and is in the habit of repeatedly dumping her negativity in my lap for an extended period, it's important for my mental and emotional health to limit my time around her. The line must be drawn somewhere.

You might feel that this is mean-spirited and that we shouldn't turn our backs on people when they want to be heard. I partially agree with that. Don't get me wrong: I am all for allowing people to share their frustrations, anger, and complaints with us. But if it becomes habitual and after multiple complaining sessions, it's clear that they have no interest in finding solutions or taking action to improve the situation, then, for your sanity, it's time to make another choice. It's the same reason I wouldn't spend hours in a car with the windows rolled up while someone is sitting shotgun smoking a pack of cigarettes.

Avoiding that situation isn't cruel; it's called survival.

Step 2: Misery Doesn't Love Company

Have you heard the statement that misery loves company? If so, it's not true. Misery doesn't love company. Misery loves *miserable* company. Chronic complainers seek out people who will validate their pain and keep them in a helpless state of inaction.

The good news is that you don't have to play that role if you don't want to.

Imagine that you have a coworker who is a constant complainer. The kind of person you're afraid to ask, "How are you?" for fear of being locked into a vortex of negativity for hours.

For example, let's say that your coworker approaches you during break time and sings the same familiar sad song to you for the fourteenth time this week:

"Ugh, I hate this place! The customers are all rude, our manager is a joke, and this company is so shady. I cannot even tell you how much I hate working here."

If you don't want to engage, or if you want to help the complainer shift into problem-solving mode, there are three ways to respond.

> **Option #1:** "Wow, that's totally not my experience at all. For the most part, I think our customers and our manager are pretty cool. Sure, this company isn't perfect. But if it weren't for them, I wouldn't be in a position to put a down payment on my new condo. Truthfully, I'm pretty happy here." (Obviously, only use this option if this is how you truly feel.)

> **Option #2:** "I hear you. You've been upset about this for a while and clearly it's having an effect on you. Let's talk about it—what's your plan to do something about it?"

> **Option #3:** "You sound really frustrated by this. What can I do to help?"

Depending on the type of chronic complainer you're dealing with, one of two things will likely happen next: He'll either make the life-saving decision to start brainstorming solutions (which is good for him), or he'll eventually leave you alone because he is not getting the response he's looking for (which is good for you).

But what if he says there's nothing he can do?

Nonsense. There is *always* something that can be done besides chronically complaining.

It is easy for a chronic complainer to dismiss this as glass-half-full optimism talk, but this is deeper than that. This is about viewing problems creatively instead of as impassable obstacles that will forever keep us from living a better life.

Overcoming obstacles makes us more valuable as employees, it makes us stronger as individuals, and it makes us better human beings and better equipped to make our workplace work.

Step 3: Ask Directly for the Complaining to Stop

Remember the secondhand smoke analogy? If someone lit up a cigarette in your car, would you just suck it up (literally and figuratively) and say nothing? It is okay to ask someone who is complaining to you to stop. For example, let's use the same example we did before with your complaining coworker:

> *Complainer:* "Ugh, I hate this place! The customers are all rude, our manager is a joke, and this company is so shady. I cannot even tell you how much I hate working here."
>
> *You:* "I know you're unhappy here, but can we talk about something else? Sitting around every afternoon during our break time and talking about how much you hate this place is a huge downer."

Here's the thing—you don't have to be anyone's emotional dumping ground unless you choose to play that role. It is okay to honor yourself by saying no to listening to complaining during your free time.

It's more than okay. It's necessary if you care about your sanity.

THE DEFINING MOMENT

If you accept the challenge of positively changing your workplace, the reward for your courage may be a kick in the teeth, a bloodied mouth, and the very real question of whether you should go on.

This is your defining moment and it should be the one that you've been waiting for. In a sense, it is your rite of passage.

Do you sit on the ground feeling sorry for yourself? Do you complain to every passerby about how much that blow hurt? Do you quit and leave this work to someone else who is better qualified? If so, I have some bad news for you: *There is no one else.* No one is coming to save you.

Or do you wipe your mouth with your sleeve, spit out the excess blood, and make the bold declaration that even though that hurt like hell, *you're still here*?

That's what a Solutionist must do.

This is a defining moment because we have choices when we inevitably get knocked down on this journey. Complain or strategize. Complain or take meaningful action. Complain or become better. Complain or lead the way. Complain or win.

The knockdown is coming—count on it. The only thing that matters is what you choose to do next.

R.E.A.L. WORK

Assignment #9:

Complaint-Free Monday

The goal of this assignment is to train your mind to creatively find solutions when faced with hardships, instead of defaulting to complaining and helplessness. To practice this, I'm asking you to go on a twenty-four-hour complaining detox, starting next Monday. Yes, that means no complaining about your professional or personal life, and no engaging in any complaint sessions with your buddies next Monday for any reason, either. By trying this just for a day, you will see how much more effective you can be when you are focused on solutions instead of complaints for twenty-four hours.

SECTION

5

THE SPIRIT

Lasting Leadership

CHAPTER

13

YOU'RE ALREADY IN CHARGE:

Leading without Authority

If your actions inspire others to dream more, learn more, do more and become more, you are a leader.

—JOHN QUINCY ADAMS

Here is, without question, the biggest mental hurdle we will need to overcome to make this movement a reality:

The idea that you can choose to be a leader right now.

You have everything you need to lead the movement to positively change your workplace. You can actually do it as soon as you are done reading this sentence. If you have positional authority (that is, you are a supervisor, a manager, a director, etc.), that is fantastic news. If you don't currently have any positional authority, and you are working toward gaining some, that's great, too. You may be reading this and have no interest in rising to a formal position of authority at your company—this is also perfectly fine.

Either way, it does not matter at all when it comes to being a leader.

Contrary to popular belief, you do not need authority over other people to be a leader. Wearing a laminated plastic badge that reads *manager* or *director* doesn't make me a leader any more than wearing a Los Angeles Lakers jersey I bought at the mall makes me a professional basketball player.

If reaching a position of authority was all it took to be considered a true leader, we're all in some serious trouble. Workplaces all over the world are full of authority figures masquerading as leaders, and I'm willing to bet that you know a few of these people.

I understand why people seek authority instead of choosing to lead with positivity. It is sexy and it nicely satisfies an ego-driven need to be in an elevated position over others. It is also much easier than doing the real work of leading with positivity.

People like this exist in every organization on earth. I used to work with a guy who proudly called his employees his "minions," and with another enlightened soul who gave herself the nickname the "Queen Bitch" and proudly declared on multiple occasions that her staff's primary reason for being at work was to obey her wishes. These people are intoxicated with the power their authority brings, and they forgot Uncle Ben's sagelike wisdom, given to a young Peter Parker before he became Spider-Man: "With great power comes great responsibility."

The problem with the people who are intoxicated by authority is that they only focus on the "great power" part of Uncle Ben's advice. With power comes control. *Because I have authority, you will do what I say because there will be negative consequences for you if you don't.* It's the simplest way to gain compliance. Similarly, if I jam a nine-millimeter gun in your ribs, I have also gained a level of authority over you. This is not leadership, even though many people in authority have fooled themselves into believing it is.

Here is the main factor that distinguishes leading with authority from leading with positivity. Ask yourself this question about anyone who currently has authority over you: If she lost her authority over you, would you still choose to follow her anyway?

The answer to this question usually says a lot. I would not be surprised if many of your current and former bosses would fail this simple test. By contrast, many people who do not have any positional authority would pass this test with flying colors.

Leadership is much more nuanced than relying solely on positional power. It's about people choosing to follow you because they want to follow you, not because they have to follow you. Put it this way: Would you feel better about being in a romantic relationship with someone who feels obligated to be with you or being in a relationship with someone who *wants to be with you?*

Obligation will get you people's bodies but never their hearts.

Having authority may put you in an ideal position to lead others, but it is not the only thing you need. I believe that you are in a better position to lead this movement without authority because you can learn to inspire action in others without relying on your title to do it for you.

This is the true core of what it means to lead with positivity.

POSITIVE LEADERSHIP, DEFINED

So, what constitutes positive leadership?

I define it as *the ability to inspire positive actions in others to reach a desired goal and collective success.*

This definition says nothing about ego-tripping over your manager title or even having a title at all. This is solely about consistently thinking, speaking, and acting in a way that will inspire positive action in others to reach a desired goal. And this is something you can do right now.

Some of the greatest leaders in history didn't have formal authority when they started on their world-altering journeys. Martin Luther King, Jr., Mahatma Gandhi, and Mother Teresa weren't corner-office executives. They didn't have tens of thousands of Twitter followers or their own reality TV shows. They did not have the ability to force anyone to do anything, and they didn't have to. They had something else that was so much more powerful:

> ***The ability to inspire positive actions in others to reach a desired goal and collective success.***

This is the part of the journey that is not for everyone. Are you sure you want to go down this road? Leading ourselves by leading by example is hard enough, but leading the process of inspiring positive change in others is much harder—and it will leave you with some unavoidable battle scars. Ask anyone who has tried to walk this path before you, and he will show them to you.

He will also say that each scar was completely worth it in the end.

The good news is this: If we follow the blueprint of the positive leaders of the past, there's no reason we can't have similar results with our movement—regardless of the challenges in our way or the authority we don't yet have.

MICHELLE'S STORY

In the 1960s Martin Luther King, Jr. had a dream of overcoming deeply ingrained racial segregation. Mahatma Gandhi had a vision of a world free from war and oppression. Mother Teresa dreamed of helping the sick and the poor all over the world. Michelle dreamed of increasing the amount of civility and appreciation in her department.

Wait, who is Michelle and why is her name in the same paragraph as Martin Luther King, Jr., Mahatma Gandhi, and Mother Teresa? While I'm sure that Michelle would be mortified to see herself compared to these visionaries, she is one of countless people who succeeded in making significant positive change in her department without any formal authority.

She worked as an administrative assistant in a marketing department, and we met in one of my workshops, where I discussed many of the topics covered in this book. Here is her story:

> *My department was not an enjoyable place to work. My boss would only speak to the staff when he needed something from us, my colleagues' primary topics of communication were either useless gossip or complaining, and the morale was in the toilet. There were no expressions of gratitude, there was very little friendly banter, there was hardly any teamwork—people just showed up, did the least amount of work possible, and then went home. Just walking into the office and sitting down in my cubicle every morning was such a draining experience that by the end of each day, I felt dead inside.*
>
> *As strange as this may sound, I was fine to continue on like this, until one day after work, as I was preparing dinner, my five-year-old daughter asked me if I was happy. It was such a strange question to be asked out of nowhere, especially by a five-year-old. Without even thinking, I robotically said, "Yes, honey," as I kept cooking without looking at her. Then she said, "You don't look happy, Mommy." That moment changed everything. Things got real in a hurry. Not only*

did I realize how unhappy I was, but I also realized that I was willing to lie to my kid in a failed attempt to hide my unhappiness. I had to do something.

I went into the office the next day, committed to make work a more meaningful experience for me. I knew that in order to make any change, I had to start with myself first by reconnecting with my Hire Self. I became crystal clear on my values, recommitted to living those values, and I focused on a small goal: getting people to be more appreciative of each other.

At our weekly team meeting, after a lot of internal debating, I spoke up and said, "You know, I don't think that we are as appreciative of each other as we should be. I want to let you know that I appreciate all of you, and I want to show you."

Before the meeting I had written out small, personalized, one-sentence statements on folded sticky notes. I pulled them out of my purse and I gave one to each of the thirteen people in the meeting, including my boss. On each note was a small expression of sincere gratitude, ranging from "Thank you for covering for me last week when my daughter was sick" to "Thank you for always brightening up the office with your smile."

I wish I could say that this moment immediately sparked a wave of positivity within my department, but that would be a flat-out lie. Some of the people looked at me as if I were insane, some chuckled uncomfortably at me, some probably felt sincerely sorry for me, and some people even threw their note in the trash after the meeting ended.

Complete positivity fail, right? Not exactly.

Two people came up to me after the meeting and hugged me. Yes, they hugged me! They told me that this was the first time they had heard "Thank you" directed at them in months, and they both had tears welling up in their eyes. We shared a moment in which we committed to making this workplace a brighter place than it was before, even if no one else but us would do it. They walked away energized and I walked away changed. That moment was the start of our mini movement.

You said it wasn't going to be easy, and it wasn't. I leaned on Gandhi's quote, "First they ignore you, then they laugh at you, then they fight you, then you win." Six months after my workshop with you and four months after that meeting, I can say that I've experienced all those things that Gandhi predicted. Even so, I stuck with it. The good part is that things have changed noticeably. Beginning with the three of us, we exemplified the workplace that we wanted to work in—an environment where we are relentlessly respectful, kind, accountable, and willing to lead by example.

Even though some people in our department may never get it, finding a group of people who are committed to making this workplace a more positive place has made it so worth it. I enjoy my work much more now, and even my daughter notices it. I never thought that I could make a difference, and I will not underestimate myself again in any area of my life.

Powerful stuff. Michelle didn't have any authority, but she still made positive change happen. She had four traits that every leader without a title needs. Consider these to be like legs on a table: If one of them is missing, the table (or, in our case, the movement) will come tumbling down in a hurry.

POSITIVE LEADERSHIP TRAIT #1: SEEING THE END (VISION)

If you truly desire to make positive change in your workplace, this is where you must start.

What's your dream?

For many people, it's simply surviving the workday without getting yelled at, without getting additional work dumped on them, and with their sanity intact. If that's your dream, that's not going to come close to cutting it. Leading yourself and others out of a broken workplace is going to require an inspiring vision. Ideally, it will be a vision of something bigger than you might think is possible.

Imagine that you're currently in a broken workplace that is full of incivility, rudeness, laziness, and a complete lack of personal accountability. Ask yourself this: What would I ideally like to see this workplace look like? Before you answer, it is important to focus your power on things that you can change. Don't say things like, "My vision is to get my boss fired." That might serve as a fun daydream, but thoughts like that will do nothing to push the movement forward.

Michelle wanted there to be more sincere appreciation in her department. What do you want to see in your workplace? Do you want more open communication between the coworkers on your team? Do you want to change the culture of overwork by working smarter instead of mindlessly putting in sixty-hour workweeks and racing your coworkers to the grave? Do you want to improve the overall morale in the department?

Regardless of what your vision may be, you must have one to inspire others to follow it. Just as with Martin Luther King, Jr. and thousands of other positive leaders of the past, the vision was the start of everything.

POSITIVE LEADERSHIP TRAIT #2: WALK THE WALK (INTEGRITY)

If inspiring positive actions in others is the goal, the quickest way to derail your goal is to say one thing and then do another.

We would not be talking about Martin Luther King, Jr. and Mahatma Gandhi if, after they created a compelling vision of changing the world through nonviolent activism, they spent their evenings getting in bar fights and smashing beer bottles over people's heads. No hypocrite ever positively changed the world, and it would serve us well to remember this.

Have you ever worked for a boss who demanded that you treat your customers with kindness and respect but treated her staff terribly? A boss who demands that you stay late to finish your work while he skates out of the office early to play a round of golf with his buddies? Speaking from personal experience, it is very hard to follow someone like that. If you care about making positive change, this is not the person you should be.

Positive leadership is impossible without leading by example. This is the heart of positive leadership, and anyone who fails to do this consistently is unfit for the title of leader. The "Do as I say but not as I do" bosses of the world are useless, destructive, and utterly incapable of inspiring excellence in anyone—including themselves.

The gift of leading by example is that you make it easy for others to follow you. It is inspiring to see someone with the guts to stand up for what's right and take action to do so.

Michelle knew this. If she wanted to make positive change without authority, she would have to walk first by speaking up in that meeting. She didn't have the luxury of simply barking out orders and having everyone follow her because she said so. She wasn't the boss. So she decided to lead in another way. In a sense, by making that declaration, she delivered a eulogy to her old self. The person who complained constantly, wasn't accountable, and hoped that someone else would do the work died in that meeting room that day.

Walking the talk is not only refreshing, but also it's inspiring. When you see someone lose excess weight, break a dysfunctional habit, become happier, or make any positive change, it's natural to want to follow his example. Walking the talk puts you effectively in the life-changing position of being a role model, and this is not a position that should be taken lightly.

If nothing else, leading by example will never be considered an exercise in failure. People are watching you. They are waiting for you to get on the dance floor first. You don't have to yell and scream like a testosterone-fueled football coach to be a strong leader. Quietly leading by example reflects much more strength because people who see you will think, "I can do this, too."

The best leaders throughout history are the ones who get people to recognize their own capacity for positive change.

POSITIVE LEADERSHIP TRAIT #3: ANCHOR IN (COMMITMENT)

Here's a quick dose of bad, but unsurprising, news.

You won't have a bikini body by going to the gym for a couple of days. You won't reach enlightenment and inner peace after fifteen minutes of meditation. You won't have better sleep, digestion, and glowing skin by drinking one kale smoothie.

But let me ask you this: Will you keep your appointment to go to the gym when it's snowing, the temperature outside is below freezing, and you are wrapped up in fuzzy blankets on the couch? Will you stick with your meditation practice when your car just broke down, your kids are acting like pint-sized terrorists, and your boss is verbally using you like his personal punching bag? Will you opt for a kale smoothie when there's a box full of cream-filled doughnuts in the break room taunting you every morning as you walk into work?

If so, that's what commitment looks like. To experience the positive changes that those activities will bring, commitment is required. There is no other path to results.

Leading this movement is no different. Dipping our toe in the water and only caring about doing the right thing when it's safe, comfortable, convenient, and easy to do so will accomplish nothing. We need to be "all in" for this to work, especially when it gets hard.

What if I told you that doing the work in this movement could take months of consistent action before you notice any positive change? What if it took longer than that? Would you still do it?

Great leaders throughout history didn't care how long it took to get results. They decided that their current circumstances were unacceptable, and even if it took them the rest of their lives, they were determined to fight for their cause. They also knew that if they stayed committed to consistent positive action, other like-minded people would see their commitment and be drawn to them. If not, at least they would be positively changed, and that would make the effort worthwhile.

Michelle stuck with it when it was hard because she had the necessary attitude to make her workplace work. Whether she knew it or not, she climbed up each step of the Attitude Adjustment Pyramid by ignoring the negative influences, expecting a challenge, identifying her values, committing to leave everything she touched better than she found it, and focusing on doing the right thing, just today. If you have ever made a positive change in your life, you likely leaned on the Attitude Adjustment Pyramid, just as Michelle did, to keep your commitment. You didn't wake up one day as a nonsmoker, in perfect physical shape, or completely out of debt. Instead, you stayed committed to doing the right thing each day and, a year later, your life was positively transformed.

If so, you have your commitment to thank for it. You will need to tap into it over and over again if you are planning to positively transform the working world.

POSITIVE LEADERSHIP TRAIT #4: HEART (COURAGE)

I don't know what was racing through Michelle's mind when she stood up in that meeting.

I can't imagine that it was easy for her to pass out handwritten notes of appreciation to people she knew would likely reject them (and some did), but she did it anyway. *That takes some serious courage.* She had no formal title to hide behind—she just stood in front of her team naked and vulnerable with only her vision to provide protection. That is a scary place to be, and I have been there.

If you are ready to take action to lead the way in your workplace, just know that it is okay to be scared. Writing this book is scary as hell for me. I don't have any formal authority, but here I am writing this book and here you are reading it. Just like Michelle, I'm done sitting on the sidelines with my ideas and waiting for some imaginary person to grant me permission to take my place as a positive leader.

Work needs to be done, and if we wait until our fears go away to do it, we might as well cancel this revolution, take our ball, and go home. It is okay to be scared to lead, but the fact that you are reading these words is all the proof I need to know that your desire is bigger than your fear. We cannot use fear as an excuse to stop us from doing what is necessary to improve the world.

Every musician, actor, athlete, and leader you admire was once a nobody racked with insecurity and self-doubt. Yes, she was scared, just as we are. *The only difference is that she acted in spite of her fear.*

This is the choice you are facing now. Be scared and lead anyway, or just be scared.

If you choose the former, remember Mahatma Gandhi's wise words that Michelle quoted earlier, "First they ignore you, then they laugh at you, then they fight you, then you win."

You will be ignored.

You will be laughed at.

You will face a fight.

Those are all guarantees. The only thing that is still in doubt is if you have the stamina, resilience, and vision to lead this movement past those challenges.

If so, you will win.

R.E.A.L. WORK

Assignment #10:

Embracing the Leader Within

Whether you have formal authority or not, now is the time for you to step into your role as a leader in this movement. Write down your vision of what you would like to see positively changed about your work team, and then write down the action you will take to lead that change. No more daydreaming and waiting for something or someone else to lead the way, Solutionist—it's on your shoulders now. Like Michelle, it could be increasing the amount of appreciation and gratitude on your team, or it could be something completely different. The key is to come up with the vision, demonstrate the necessary integrity by walking the talk, stay committed to the vision when it gets hard, and, most of all, have the courage to lead the way. Title or not, you are a leader. Embrace that.

CHAPTER

14

INVISIBLE NO MORE:

Valuing Everyone

Everyone has an invisible sign hanging from their neck saying "Make me feel important." Never forget this message when working with people.

—MARY KAY ASH

Many years ago, as I was leaving the office late one night, I ran into an executive leader in my former workplace.

"Hey, Shola, good to see you," he said as he shook my hand and continued down the hallway.

On his way out of the building, he literally bumped into a woman who was entering the building as he was exiting. He didn't even break stride, he didn't say, "Excuse me," he just kept going as if she weren't even there. I'm not sure if I would have believed the rudeness if I hadn't seen it with my own eyes.

The woman he bumped into was named Patty, and she was a part of the building's janitorial staff. I came to know her because, just like me, she was a huge basketball fan, so we would always talk about our favorite teams whenever I stayed late enough to see her. Her smile was so engaging that it lit up a room.

But that night was different.

Moments after that bump incident, Patty's demeanor changed. She sat down in a nearby chair in our now completely empty lobby, and shook her head dejectedly. My heart broke for this woman, and I took my bag off my shoulder and sat down beside her to ask what was wrong, even though I already knew the answer.

"I have been responsible for cleaning that man's office every night for the past two years, and he has never said a word to me when he sees me," she said with her voice shaking with both anger and sadness, "No 'Hi,' no 'How are you?' Nothing. He just bumped into me on his way out of the building, and he still didn't even say anything. It's like I'm invisible to him."

Invisible.

Have you ever felt invisible? Have you ever felt as if you do not matter, as if you are unimportant? I've been there. If you have, too, you don't need me to tell you how much it hurts.

Almost everyone can relate to feeling insignificant, and I am confident that most people can relate to leaders who, intentionally or unintentionally, make people feel insignificant through their actions and words.

The simple and obvious truth is that everyone is important. When people feel unimportant and unvalued, that is usually when the cracks in the foundation begin to form.

This is not how to lead this movement.

THE SEDUCTIVE LEADERSHIP TRAP

Whether you are a leader with authority or without it, there is one seductive trap that you cannot allow yourself to stumble into if you care about creating a more positive world: *the idea that some jobs, some roles, and some people are more important than others.*

This is insanity of the highest order.

Is your left eye more important than your right hand? Is the second baseman more important than the center fielder? Is the violinist more important than the trombonist? Is the woman who runs the business *really* more important than the guy who cleans the business? It's time to stop splitting hairs and remember the only truth that matters:

Everyone is important.

Everyone plays an important role and unless everyone works at maximum capacity the whole team is at heightened risk of failure.

Even worse, placing levels of importance on people puts you at risk of the dreaded "better than" complex.

Sadly, I have seen countless leaders from all walks of life who act as if they are better than the people they are entrusted to lead.

I have seen newly promoted supervisors who refuse to help out on the front lines because that work is beneath them now. I have seen managers who don't even care to know the full names of the people on their team. I have seen directors who wouldn't even dream of listening to an idea that came from an employee who is two levels below their pay grade. I have seen physicians who act as if you are unworthy of breathing the same air they do unless you are rocking a white coat, as they are. I have seen an executive shoulder-block an unsuspecting janitor and not a say a word of apology afterward.

Why does this happen so often with leaders in the modern workplace?

I have heard all the excuses: It's due to the fast-paced nature of the workplace. It's because leaders don't have the time to make people feel important. It's because their minds are too preoccupied with the stresses of leadership.

Seriously, do you buy any of that foolishness? I don't. These are not even close to being acceptable reasons to act like an ass.

So why do leaders often act as if they are better than their direct reports? My opinion is that it's not important enough to them to act otherwise. I would be willing to wager next month's mortgage payment that the executive would have paused to apologize if he had shoulder-blocked his boss or his mother on his way out of the office.

There is a huge danger in choosing to lead with the idea that some people and some roles are important and some aren't.

The ones who feel marginalized are far less likely to put forth their best effort, sacrifice for the team, or care very much. Be honest—would you consistently give your best to a leader who made you feel invisible, insignificant, and ignored? Would you fight for a leader who didn't give a damn whether you lived or died? Would you be fully engaged to work for a leader who was unwilling to give you the basic respect and kindness that he would likely give to his pet gerbil?

I wouldn't. These leaders are the ones who have failed us and the rest of the working world for too long. Remember in chapter 8 where I said that you need to own the change before you're shown the change when it comes to making friends? It's the same thing with positive leadership. If you want to see commitment from the people you are leading, you must show that you are committed to them first. Remembering that we are all wearing an invisible sign that says *Make me feel important* is an excellent start.

Even though the sign might be invisible, our job as leaders is to ensure that no person feels unimportant.

If you are a leader with authority or you're working toward becoming a leader with authority, here are five ways to lead so that never happens.

1. Valuing Their Ideas

One of the key goals of any positive leader is to create more leaders, and one of the easiest ways to do that is to value the ideas of the staff and give them control over their work environment.

The best ideas will always come from the people who are closest to the work. This seems obvious, but there are many companies spending hundreds of thousands of dollars (or more) on consultants with advanced degrees to come up with ideas they could have gotten for free just by talking to the staff. Even worse, by ignoring the ideas of the staff, they lose a key opportunity to inspire and engage the staff and help them to own their work by showing that their opinions matter.

Weak leaders care about where an idea comes from, rather than the quality of the idea itself.

If you are in the role of supervising others, this isn't about placing a suggestion box in the break room and then calling it a day. This is about having the challenging discussions and asking the difficult questions.

- *What are the most common concerns that you're hearing from our customers, and how do you think we can address those concerns?*
- *Is there anything you need from me to do your job more effectively?*
- *What could we be doing better?*

- *If there was one thing that started happening (or stopped happening) in our department right now that would have a positive effect on your overall engagement, what would that be?*

These questions are a powerful way to begin a useful dialogue, and to ensure that employees feel in control of their work environment. Of course, if you are planning to ask the difficult questions, you need to have the guts to listen to the equally difficult answers. Saying that you value the ideas, but then routinely ignoring those ideas is like pouring hydrochloric acid on your employees' morale.

As a positive leader, you won't be able to implement every suggestion you hear, but you can ensure that the people making those suggestions know why you are unable to incorporate their ideas, if you can't.

Your people will not feel invisible if you show them that you value their ideas.

2. Valuing Their Work

I wish that I could have asked the executive who routinely ignored Patty the janitor these two simple questions:

1. If you don't feel that Patty and her job are important, why do you pay her to do it?
2. Do you routinely hire insignificant people to do work that doesn't matter? If so, you really have no business being in an executive role.

I can guarantee you that Patty would become *very* important to him if she decided not to empty his trash can every night and his office started to smell like a landfill. But seriously, it is beyond shameful that it would require Patty *not to do her job* for that executive to realize the value of her work.

Thankfully, I have been blessed to work with many executives who do get it and deeply value the work of the people they are entrusted to lead. My dear friend Christina is a health-care executive who is a rock-star leader in every sense of the word. I could write an entire chapter on her leadership skills, but one of the many areas in which she is exceptional is in showing her team how much she values their work.

Even though she is an executive, she routinely jumps in to cover the front desk at one of the many medical practices she oversees when they are short-staffed. Think of the executives you have worked with throughout your career. Would they jump on the phone at the call center? Would they bag groceries at the supermarket? Would they wait tables at the restaurant? If so, then I know two things about those executives: They are universally loved and they value the work of the front line.

Christina understands this fully. Her actions send a clear message that everyone's role is important and there is no work that is beneath her. Predictably, she has created a legend for herself in which people will happily do anything that she asked of them, and all it took to reach legend status is to consistently value the work of her entire team.

Our job is to emulate her. People feel more engaged in their work when they feel their work is recognized and valued.

There are no physicians without nurses, there are no pilots without flight attendants, there are no restaurant owners without the waitstaff, there are no lawyers without paralegals, there are no CEOs without the dedication of the front line.

Most importantly, your people will not feel invisible if you show them that you value their work.

3. Valuing Their Time

Leaders overlook this at their own peril. When you don't respect people's time, you make them feel unimportant and unvalued.

I used to work for a leader who would have her assistant schedule me for one-on-one meetings, and then keep me waiting in the hallway outside her office for twenty to thirty minutes past our scheduled meeting time. Then she'd have her assistant sheepishly cancel the meeting after I had wasted all that time waiting for her. This happened often, and needless to say, I did not feel very important or valued when I worked for her.

As a leader, valuing people's time isn't simply about starting and ending meetings on time. It is about ensuring that you are fully present during the time you spend with your people. Swiping through your cell phone, answering emails, and sending texts while you are meeting with your employees is a disrespectful and unprofessional habit. As a positive leader, the ability to stay present and focused on the person in front of you is a game-changer, and it's something that many weaker leaders are unable to do.

Remember, time is the most valuable resource in the world. It cannot be borrowed, multiplied, or given back after you lose it. *It can only be spent.* Do so wisely.

Your people will not feel invisible if you show them that you value their time.

4. Valuing Their Ability

When leaders micromanage, they demoralize their teams and prompt superstar employees to jump ship to another company.

Maybe you've worked for one of these micromanagers. It's the boss who wants you to "cc" him on every email you send, just to check that you are giving out the correct information. It's the boss who wants a detailed report at the end of each day to show her exactly how you spent every minute of your day. It's the boss who gives you an assignment to complete and keeps asking for constant updates long before the deadline. It's the boss who will not allow you to make the most basic decisions without running them by him first.

Leaders who routinely show that they do not trust their employees' abilities to complete the simplest tasks are asking for trouble. Not only does this leadership style completely stifle creativity and productivity, but it also disempowers employees, it makes them more dependent on the boss, and it wastes everyone's time.

Worst of all, this complete lack of trust in other people can even make a superstar employee second-guess her own abilities. In many cases, micromanaged employees start to feel so small and insignificant that they begin to feel invisible.

If you are entrusted to lead others, trust those people to do their jobs without your constant supervision. Positive leaders do not expect perfection from their staff. They expect that mistakes will be made and that their employees will learn from those mistakes.

But your people won't learn if you are hovering over them and salivating over every opportunity to point out the most minor of mistakes. If you want to keep your best and your brightest around (and believe me, you do), and make sure they feel like important members of the team, this is a leadership habit that must be eradicated quickly.

Your people will not feel invisible if you show them that you value their abilities.

5. Valuing the People

I've saved the most important point for last.

Some leaders feel that there must be a ten-foot high wall between them and their employees. They live in constant fear that they will be taken advantage of if they don't keep their employees at arm's length. I have never understood the point of doing that, because it is such an ineffective leadership strategy.

In my workshops, I ask employees, "What are the main things that a leader could do to help you feel more valued as a person?" Here are the three most common things I have heard in response:

1. **Say Hello.** This seems so simple, but it is shocking how often leaders fail to do this. Simply saying hello, as a way of genuinely acknowledging others, has such a powerful effect on people. Look them in the eye, refer to them by their name, and smile. I don't care how busy you are, you have time to do this. On the flip side, the amount of goodwill that is lost by ignoring people and not saying hello is incalculable.

2. **Have Their Backs.** Another beautiful way to make people feel important is to have their back when customers, clients, or other colleagues are acting abusively toward them. Dealing with difficult and rude people is part of many jobs, but when someone crosses the line and becomes verbally abusive (for instance, insulting someone's personal appearance, angrily cursing at someone, or making a racist or sexist comment), it means a lot to know that you are unwilling to accept that type of behavior toward your people. Losing an abusive customer is far less important than losing the respect of your team.

3. **Connect on a Personal Level.** The people who work for you are not easily replaced widgets. Those days are over. These are human beings who want to know that you care about them and their overall well-being.

Employees have hopes, dreams, and fears. They will experience the birth of their first child. They will experience breakups and divorces. They will have kids who will graduate from kindergarten, high school, and college. They will suffer injuries and accidents. They will get married. They will experience the death of loved ones. In other words, they will go through all the ups and downs that are part of the human experience—and all these things will affect their work performance in one way or another.

Weak leaders won't care about any of this, but the positive leader will. Genuinely caring about your employees, including knowing their kids' names, isn't weird, creepy, or intrusive—it's good business. It shows they mean more to you than what they can do for you in the workplace.

Your people will not feel invisible if you show them that you value them as people.

I CAN SEE YOU NOW

Chances are if you have accepted your role as a leader in this movement, it is because you intimately know the pain of working in an environment in which people are not fully valued. The people who are marginalized feel invisible, and invisible people don't feel as if they can make a positive impact on the world.

To make the workplace work, we need to change that, forever.

Everyone is important, everyone can have a meaningful impact, and everyone deserves to be seen, heard, and valued.

R.E.A.L. WORK
Assignment #11:

Value Statements

For this assignment, the goal is to actively demonstrate how much you value your colleagues and/or your staff. Write down how you will personally show that you value others in each of the following five areas:

1. Their ideas
2. Their work
3. Their time
4. Their ability
5. Them as people

As always, leaving these ideas on a page is meaningless. Once you have come up with a way to value others in each of those five areas, take the necessary steps to put these ideas into action. You might help someone who feels invisible to finally feel visible again.

CHAPTER

15

DEATH BEFORE LIFE:

Becoming a Leader Who Will Change the World

I don't know what your destiny will be, but one thing I know: The ones among you who will be really happy are those who have sought and found how to serve.

—ALBERT SCHWEITZER

I know a lot of people who are fascinated by the concept of life after death. I am not one of them. I find it much more meaningful to explore the concept of death before life.

On the surface, those sentences may look like two different ways to say the same thing, but they're not even close. One is focused on what happens after we die, while the other is focused on what we need to do to truly live. To live fully and lead this movement, many of us will need to die. Also, to raise the stakes a little, our deaths will need to come at our own hands.

That is the secret that I have been holding back from sharing with you until now.

Everything that you have read up to this point has been strategically laid out with one primary goal in mind:

I want you to kill yourself.

I'm speaking figuratively, of course, but that doesn't mean I'm not serious about this. If you have read all the previous chapters, you know I'm not asking you to make some minor tweaks to your personal style or to try out one of these strategies for a day or two, then quit. That halfhearted commitment has kept us stuck in this mess for decades.

If you are still here and you still want to walk down the challenging path to lead this movement, real sacrifices will have to be made—*starting with killing the old you.*

What does that mean in a practical sense?

For starters, no longer can you be anything less than fully accountable to yourself and to your work. No longer can you allow your mood to determine your manners and show up to work with a miserable attitude. No longer can you sit back and wait for a hero to step in to address the ABCs of your workplace. No longer can you cling to the excuses that will stop you from guarding your priorities, your health, and your sanity. No longer can you believe that you need the title of manager, director, or CEO to lead this movement. No longer can you wait another moment to do the real work of positively changing yourself, your workplace, and, ideally, your world.

If there is part of you—even if it is a small part—that is unwilling to do the work specified in the previous paragraph, it is up to you to find that part of yourself and kill it. Today. Better yet, right now.

Not everyone is willing to make sacrifices, and I understand this fully. The barrier to entry as a leader in this movement must be high, and it is: If we want to experience something different, we must be willing to do things differently. Sacrifice is one of those things.

I haven't even mentioned the biggest sacrifice yet.

THE NEW FOCAL POINT

To lead this movement, we will have to give up one big thing: *being the primary focus.*

The people we are leading are our focus now, and it is up to us to serve them in the best way possible. In other words, as leaders of this movement, our primary objective is not to place our own needs and desires first; our main goal is to put the needs and desires of our followers first.

This is not a new concept by any stretch. In 1970, management consultant and author Robert Greenleaf published an influential essay, titled "The Servant as Leader," which brought the term *servant leadership* into the vernacular. Leaders who make our workplaces work lead by serving others first.

Although servant leadership is a widely respected leadership philosophy, it is shocking to see how many leaders believe in leading in the opposite manner. They think that leadership means their followers work for them. That is not true, and the most positive leaders in the world know this. They work for their followers—not only because without followers they cannot be leaders, but also because doing so is the quickest way for the leaders to maximize their positive impact on the world. Leading by serving creates others who are more willing to lead by serving.

Leadership in its purest form is not a position; it is a responsibility. Let's leave the bloviating, loud-mouthed, "Hey look at me and my fancy job title" silliness for the wannabes stuck at the kiddie end of the leadership table. In the meantime, we'll be busy rolling up our sleeves, doing the work to positively change our workplaces and the world. Solutionists lead by being servants first.

Does this sound like a sacrifice you are ready and willing to make? For the people who are ready to lead in this way, it won't be that much of a sacrifice at all. If you are ready, it starts by living the R.E.A.L. philosophy detailed in the previous chapters and by being real ourselves in order to fully connect with others.

Connecting with others is how we will best serve the world.

THE SECRET OF CONNECTION: BEING PERFECTLY IMPERFECT

Do you have a friend or someone you follow on social media who appears to be perfect? You know who I'm talking about.

It's the mom who proudly (and frequently) tells all her online "friends" that her four-year-old son has never had a temper tantrum, can speak five different languages fluently, and regularly makes the family breakfast in bed. It is the guy who wakes up at 3:00 a.m. every morning to get in a "quick" ten-mile run before putting in a full day at his six-figure job, has abs that you can grate cheese on, and gets his boundless energy from solely eating kale chips, drinking alkaline water, and breathing in the infinite power of the universe.

Can you relate to these people? I can't. No one can relate to the person who has it all together, because *no one* has it all together. The quickest way to dash any hope of creating a deep connection with other people is to act as if you are perfect.

This is doubly important to remember as a leader. Once you have created an image of yourself that others cannot relate to, you have lost the ability to truly reach them. And if you can't reach them, you can't lead them. Putting on the veneer of perfection is not only ineffective, but also it's exhausting, unsustainable, a complete lie, and makes us boring. Perfection destroys connections, and it has no place in leadership.

As a leader, the goal is not to appear perfect. *The goal is to be real.* This worries some people. Does being real mean sharing our weaknesses? Does that mean admitting our mistakes? Does that mean refusing to hide our insecurities and acknowledging that we're scared?

Ideally, yes, to all of it.

No, you don't have to share your deepest, darkest personal and professional insecurities and private failings in a weekly, companywide email newsletter. But, on the flip side, you don't have to frantically hide and minimize your flaws on a daily basis in a failed attempt to appear perfect, either. The positive leader must find a happy medium.

The happy medium is doing whatever it takes to create a deeper connection with your followers. If you only care about having people's bodies behind you, all you will need is a title. But if you care about having people's hearts and minds behind you as well, you will need much more than authority. You will need to build deep connections by leading in a way that many people (including your old self) are unwilling to do.

We must be willing to be authentic and vulnerable.

There is a risk in doing this, and since I have talked a lot about leading by example, I will walk first.

GETTING *REALLY* REAL

Dr. Brené Brown, a researcher, a college professor, and an author (and one of the people I am committed to meeting in person before I die), said in her TED talk, *Listening to Shame*, "Vulnerability is our most accurate measurement of courage." I cannot agree with her more on this point.

Dr. Brown defines vulnerability in her best-selling book, *Daring Greatly* as "uncertainty, risk, and emotional exposure."*1* Sounds pretty scary, doesn't it? It should, because it *is* scary. Sadly, that's why so many leaders avoid vulnerability, because they are scared to look weak and unfit for their leadership role.

What those leaders are missing is that the risk of being vulnerable comes with extremely high rewards: loyalty, commitment, and, most of all, trust. Being loved is great, but many people love people they don't trust. There is no higher honor that one human being can bestow on another than saying, "I trust you." It does not matter if it is in the break room, the boardroom, or the bedroom, vulnerability and trust are the cornerstones to creating deeply satisfying relationships.

Because I believe wholeheartedly in vulnerability, I want to put myself out there.

To help clear my thoughts during the process of writing this book, I engaged in regular journaling exercises. I'm going to share a private journal entry I wrote when I first starting writing the book you are reading now.

> *Right now, it is the middle of the night as I'm typing this at my kitchen table, and my mind is being ravaged by my self-doubts and insecurities. I am exhausted, I don't feel like writing anymore, and worst of all, I feel as if my insecurities are starting to win. My self-criticism is louder now than I can ever remember hearing it. Here is what I'm hearing as I sit down to write:*
>
> *"Who are you to write about a workplace positivity movement? You're not Martin Luther King, Jr. Get over yourself. This book is going to end up as another example of literary roadkill that will be forgotten about as soon as you're done writing it. People with more influence in*

> *their little toe than you have in your entire body have failed miserably to positively change the workplace in any meaningful way. You don't belong in the same breath as them. The beginning of this chapter to this point has taken you 4½ hours to write. That's pathetic. What author takes 4½ hours to write fewer than 800 words? Go to bed and stop wasting your time. You're not built for this and you never have been."*
>
> *That's what I'm dealing with. I know I've been bullied before and I have dealt with self-worth issues my entire life, but this time it seems different. This time the bullies seem stronger than me and better equipped to take me down. I can't call for help, I can't run, and I can't hide because the bullies are in my head. For the first time, I am willing to admit that I might not be cut out for this. I am scared as hell because I can't turn back now, even if I wanted to. People are counting on me to deliver, but I'm not sure if I have what it takes. Whoever has believed in me has made a big mistake placing their faith in me.*

After typing those words, with tears in my eyes, I shut my laptop and stopping writing for nearly two months.

The good news is that my insecurities did not stop me or else this book wouldn't have made it into your hands. Still, though, the war rages on in my mind, and every day is a battle to prove to myself that I am worthy of doing this work. Enough about me—I have a question for you. Is it possible that you read that journal excerpt and thought less of me than you did before you read it?

Of course it is. I mean, come on—the image of a grown-ass 6-foot-2-inch, 215-pound man sobbing over his laptop at his kitchen table in the middle of the night while he battles his inner insecurities is pretty pathetic, isn't it? It's possible that I could lose a few cool points for that.

Here's the thing. *I don't give a damn about cool points.* Being cool is one of the most overrated pursuits in history. I'm here to fight through my insecurities, stare down my fears, and lead this movement to the end.

Here's what is interesting, though. Maybe you read that journal entry and felt closer to me now than you did before you read it. Our bond as Solutionists might be stronger now because you know that I'm dealing each day with the exact same challenges, insecurities, doubts, and fears as you are feeling as a leader in this movement. If you felt alone before, you now know that you're not—we're in this together and we always have been.

Don't think that because I'm writing this book I have some special talent or ability. I'm not special. I'm struggling the same way as everyone else on this planet. My talent, if you want to call it one, is that I keep showing up to do the work. What I am doing, anyone else can do, too.

We can't let our struggles define us—we are all struggling in one way or another—but do you have the courage to admit that as a leader? It is okay to admit that you do not have all the answers. It is okay to say you're sorry and admit that you were wrong. It is okay to admit that you made a bad decision. It is okay to admit that you failed.

Are there risks in doing those things? Sure there are. But they do not come close to the risks of feigning perfection, giving our insecurities the final say over the direction of our lives, or quitting when the struggle becomes too difficult. Being imperfect is an unavoidable aspect of the human condition, and there is no amount of playing it cool that will protect you from experiencing it. As a leader in this movement, your job is to deal with this reality, not hide from it.

Vulnerability doesn't make you appear weak, as many insecure, ego-driven leaders believe. Real strength comes from facing our struggles, and choosing to act in spite of them. It shows others that they are not struggling alone, and that it is possible for us to keep fighting to overcome our imperfections, while still leading this movement.

That is not a sign of weakness. That's inspiring.

Keep that in mind, because we are going to need that inspiration sooner rather than later.

WHO ARE YOU FIGHTING FOR?

In its purest form, a movement consists of a group of people who are inspired around a shared idea and, together, they commit to turning that idea into something bigger and more significant. A great deal of this book has been focused on how to inspire ourselves and others to do just that.

Connection is the common element in every successful movement. Famous movements in our country's history, such as the women's suffrage movement and the civil rights movement, serve as excellent examples of this. Members of these movements didn't see the other members as random strangers—they were brothers and sisters. They looked into the eyes of the men and women standing next to them and they saw themselves. When they fought to advance the movement, they weren't doing it solely for personal gain: They were fighting for the people who stood beside them, too. That is the power of connection.

Just like every other successful movement that paved the way before us, we need to tap into that connection if we're going to make a significant difference. Whether we are trying to change the world or our department at work, we will not be able to sustain the passion to keep fighting unless we are fighting for more than ourselves.

Here is who I am fighting for. I am fighting for the person who has given up hope that her career can be saved. She is surrounded by rudeness, incivility, and bullying on a daily basis and she does not see any way out. She desperately needs her job because she is living paycheck to paycheck, and she has a family to support and a mortgage to pay. Her health is declining, her relationships are eroding, and her sanity is fading rapidly. She feels lost, trapped, alone, and terrified that the pain she is experiencing will continue indefinitely. If there was hope, she would happily cling to it; instead, she cries herself to sleep, searching for a light that she is unable to find.

I lose sleep thinking about this person.

Something powerful happens once you become clear about who you are fighting for. The fears that come with being vulnerable and authentic become instantly meaningless. Does it really matter that some misguided haters will mistake our vulnerability for weakness? Let them. What is much scarier is failing to serve our struggling brothers and sisters by allowing our egos and insecurities to keep us disconnected from them. We can't let that happen.

Leadership is not about putting our own needs first. We are here to serve the needs of those who need us.

Are you ready to make this sacrifice, even if it means killing off the old you to make it happen? If so, remember this—there is nothing positive about destroying something unless you are able to put something better in its place.

I believe that the *something better* is the leader you are destined to become.

R.E.A.L. WORK
Assignment #12:

Killing the Old You

For this final assignment, the goal is to effectively kill off the old version of yourself—or, more specifically, the parts of you that are getting in your way. Whether it's a fear of being vulnerable, an unwillingness to engage in assertive conversations, a bad attitude, an inability to set boundaries, a tendency to complain instead of finding solutions, or something else, now is the time to face them squarely. Write down the habits that are standing in the way of you becoming the leader you need to be, and the behaviors you will put in their place. Then share both those lists with your Solutionist Society. Staying accountable for getting rid of bad habits is a very tricky process, and it is worthwhile to enlist the help of your friends on this life-enhancing journey.

SECTION

6

A NEW REALITY

The Road Ahead

CHAPTER

16

WHEN KEEPING IT R.E.A.L. GOES WRONG:

Knowing When to Quit

Quitting is not giving up, it's choosing to focus your attention on something more important. Quitting is letting go of things (or people) that are sucking the life out of you so you can do more things that will bring you strength.

—OSAYI OSAR-EMOKPAE

I remember standing in my boss's office on my very first day of work, in my first-ever job after graduating from college, in total shock at what he had just asked me to do.

It was a small business, there was no Human Resources Department available to assist me—I was just a twenty-two-year-old kid whose only professional experience was working in a fast food restaurant, in a shoe store at the mall, and as a basketball camp counselor. Even so, there is no amount of professional experience that would have prepared me for what happened on that day.

My boss, who had not been involved in the interview process for some reason, leaned back in his chair and matter-of-factly said that he didn't like the name *Shola* because it was "too complicated and weird" for his customers to pronounce. Yes, seriously. I still remember how he said that, too. Disgust dripped off each word: *too complicated and weird*. Crazy, right? Hang in there because there's more.

That is when he reached into his desk, pulled out a name badge, and tossed it to me. I caught it and looked at it with confusion because my name wasn't on the name badge. It read STEVE instead.

Noticing my confusion, he informed me that while I'm at work he wanted me to refer to myself as "Steve," instead of "Shola." Oh, and if I wasn't okay with this impromptu name change, I would need to find myself another job, effective immediately. You read that right.

So, here I was as a twenty-two-year-old kid, faced with my first-ever major career decision. I could either walk out of that dump with my head held high with my "complicated and weird" West African name, or I could clip my new name badge onto my crisp brand-new suit and get to work.

The decision was obvious, right? Well, not for me, it wasn't. Within minutes, I walked out of his office, pitifully rocking my new name badge, which I wore in quiet shame for the entire time I worked there.

If the story ended at this point, you would have my complete permission to drop this book in the nearest trash can because I wouldn't be worthy of your time or respect.

Don't worry, it doesn't.

Thankfully, this is when the story begins.

Three days into my new job, I struck up a conversation with a customer, and as she was leaving, she glanced down at my name tag and said, "Thanks for your help, Steve. I really appreciate everything you've done for me."

Without even thinking, I said, "Actually, my name is Shola."

With a look of slight confusion and sincere curiosity, she said, "That's such a beautiful name! Why does your name tag say 'Steve' on it?"

I stood there in stunned silence. It was such a simple question, but it was also one that I was completely unable to answer.

Did my name tag say STEVE on it because the fear of turning off my customers with my real name was scarier to me than losing my dignity?

Did my name tag say STEVE because I had left my manhood at home and I couldn't stand up to my boss, who was so clearly in the wrong?

Did my name tag say STEVE because my self-respect wasn't nearly as valuable to me as the $14.50/hour the company was paying me?

The questions that swirled in my mind only added to my confusion. I still remained silent as the woman waited patiently for an answer to a question that should have been incredibly easy to answer. Finally, with tears welling up in my eyes, I gave her the only answer that made any sense:

"I don't know."

At that moment I felt *it* for the first time in my life.

Seconds later, I gave the customer a hug and thanked her (she had no idea why I did either of those things), I ripped the name tag off my chest as I stomped through the store, burst into my boss's office while he was on the phone on a personal call, threw the name tag at him, and yelled "I QUIT!" as loudly as I could so that everyone within one hundred yards could hear it.

Was this my proudest professional moment? Not by a long shot.

Do I regret doing it? Not for a millisecond.

After I threw my name tag at my boss, I remember him saying, "Steve, you're a quitter who just proved that you won't amount to anything. You don't have what it takes to thrive in a workplace like this."

He was half right.

THE PAIN OF NEVER AGAIN

In case you're wondering, you don't need to have your boss threaten to fire you if you don't change your name, or be on the brink of suicide, as I was (as chronicled in the introduction), in order to decide to quit. You do need to know your breaking point, though.

Remember, in the story about my first job, I said that I felt *it* for the first time in my life? What I was referring to was my professional and personal breaking point or, as I like to call it, my "never again" point.

Have you ever had something happen to you that was so horrific, so unbearable, and so intensely destructive to your spirit that you were convinced from that moment forward that you would *never* experience that pain again?

If so, that's what I'm talking about. You intimately know the pain of "never again."

Just to be clear: This is not about being yelled at or being asked to work on a Saturday when you already had plans. This is about wildly egregious behavior that no sane person should ever have to endure in a professional environment, much less accept. I can't draw that line for you, so I will leave it to you to do that. But, please, when your never-again point is crossed, you must honor yourself by ensuring that you *never* subject yourself that kind of abuse again.

THE THREE OPTIONS TO SAVE YOUR CAREER

Now that we have that ugliness out of the way, you might be in a situation that is far less extreme than the one outlined, but you are still absolutely miserable in your job. What do you do then?

If you are in that place right now, there are only three positive options available to you if you want to move forward with your life while working in a less-than-positive work environment: *Get in, get up, or get out.*

Positive Choice #1: Get In

This simply means that, despite the challenges, drama, and difficult personalities you are currently facing, you believe that you can create positive change. You are going "all in" on the R.E.A.L. philosophy and on doing the work of positively changing your workplace, regardless of the time and effort it will take to make it happen. This entire book is about getting in.

You might be in a situation in which quitting isn't an option. Maybe you are a single parent, you have rent or a mortgage to pay, you are living from paycheck to paycheck and have nothing in your savings account, or all of the above. After reading this far, hopefully you've been given tools to renew your dedication to fight for your career. This means that you are in, and if you are in, remember that many people are willing to fight beside you. You are not alone. The challenges of choosing this path have already been laid out in the previous chapters, so I won't rehash them here. Just know that choosing this path can positively change the world.

Positive Choice #2: Get Up

This option is slightly different from getting in, but it is just as powerful, and it worked for me.

If you are so sick and tired of how the leaders in your company are leading you, then it is time to get up. If you feel that the fastest way to gain influence in your situation is to gain positional power to make the changes happen, commit to making that happen. Go back to school, take some supervisory classes or attend seminars, read leadership books or watch leadership videos, apply for any leadership job you are qualified for (and some that you are not), or simply become a better version of yourself.

Whatever it takes, if you feel that the answer is to get up, by all means, do it.

Positive Choice #3: Get Out

Here's an assumption that I am going to make about you. You are the type of person who has a bias toward fighting for yourself and your career, and you don't willingly roll over once the going gets tough. I need to know this about you, because that is the sign of a true Solutionist and the sign of the person you must be in order to positively change the working world. As you know, the road ahead of you is not an easy one.

But I'm not naive. This is not a decision to be taken lightly. In certain situations, getting out is the only positive option that makes sense. If you are in a position in which you can't quit for whatever reasons (say, financial reasons), choose to either get in or get up while you're busy plotting your exit strategy.

If you are still unsure as to whether getting out is the best option for you, let's dive more deeply into it.

THE GET OUT CHECKLIST

This is not about running from your problems. Choosing to quit is not an easy decision to make, but take a look at the nine-point checklist that starts on the next page and see how many of them are part of your current situation. If you say yes to more than half the items, it might be time for you to get out.

1. Your Health Is Negatively Affected

In situations in which you are so miserable, so broken, so close to a nervous breakdown every day you show up at the workplace, it's probably time to get out. If you do not have your physical, mental, and emotional health working for you, you will never be your best in any area of your life. Toxic jobs can kill you, and this is not said metaphorically. As previously noted, toxic jobs have been known to contribute to heart conditions, ulcers, migraine headaches, strokes, depression, post-traumatic stress disorder, relapse into harmful addictions, just to name a few. In extreme situations, some people felt so hopeless as a result of their job situation that they considered suicide. As you know, I've been there and it isn't pretty. These ailments should not be ignored or rationalized away. If you have reached the point at which your mental and physical health are declining on a daily basis, you have a very important decision to make. You only get one shot at this life, and no job or relationship is ever worth sacrificing your health for it.

2. Your Personal Relationships Are Negatively Affected

This is the saddest outcome of all, in my opinion. I know of many marriages that ended in divorce, parents who have strained relationships with their kids, and people who have lost contact with their friends and family because of the stress of the job. Ironically, many people stay in miserable jobs for their loved ones, but staying in that toxic job is the primary thing that is driving a wedge into their relationship. Sadly, many people take out their stress at the job on the people who are on their side and who least deserve their wrath. In cases like this, a toxic job spreads its toxic effects into other aspects of life. Not only do you hate your life at the office, but also your workplace is sapping the joy out of your personal life as well.

3. You Have Changed for the Worse

You have gained weight. You started smoking as a form of stress relief. You are irritable and snap at people at a moment's notice. You used to care so much about being the best version of yourself, but now you can barely find the motivation to iron your clothes, brush your teeth, and take care of yourself. Smiling used to come naturally to you, but now it's like being asked to run a half marathon on a bed of nails. If any of this sounds like you, ask yourself: Have I changed for the worse and am I okay with living the rest of my life as the person I am now?

4. You Are Completely Alone

When you go to work every day and you notice that there is no one you like or respect on the job, you have a problem on your hands. This is going to require some self-awareness, though. One of my mentors used to say, "If you go outside and run across an asshole, he's likely an asshole. But if you go outside and *everyone* you see is an asshole, unfortunately, you're probably the asshole." If you've checked yourself and feel confident that you're not the problem, and you are currently wading through a sea of gossipers, backstabbers, and self-preservationists who would happily throw you under the bus to win favor with the boss, it might be time to go. Even worse, if you work for a small company that doesn't have a Human Resources Department or any other recourse when you need help, you are in a very precarious spot.

5. Your Boss Is a Nightmare and Isn't Going Anywhere

If you are working for a boss who treats you in a subhuman fashion, but she babysits her boss's kids on the weekend and is family friends with the CEO, you are in for an uphill battle. There are many awful bosses who have turned their ability to "manage up" into an art form. They bring in the numbers and make their bosses look great, which gives them the necessary cover to treat their staff in any matter that they see fit. If you don't respect your boss, and this person has created a network of strategically advantageous relationships to protect her, that could be a problem for you. However, wrong is wrong, so I'm not afraid to stand up against this behavior. Some people are not willing to do that. Either way, just know that if you are in this situation, it is not going to be easy to deal with.

6. You Are Embarrassed about Where You Work

Sometimes we end up in jobs with companies that are ethically and morally bankrupt, with public reputations that are so bad you are literally ashamed to work there. That's how I felt with the job that I described in the introduction. People who work there take off their badges when they go out of the office for lunch because they don't want anyone to know they work there. The turnover is ridiculously bad—in ninety days, you will be working with a completely different staff. And those who survived and quit wonder why it took them so long to leave. I'm out of that job more than a decade and on my Facebook page, I still see people exhibiting a form of Stockholm syndrome as they pitifully try to justify the atrocities that place is heaping on them. I understand the need to collect a paycheck, but exchanging your dignity for it is not a fair trade-off.

7. You Have No Passion for the Job and/or You Are Unchallenged

It is human nature to want to grow and get better. Having passion for the work you are doing will help you grow quickly, but if your passion is nonexistent, most likely, so is your growth. Even worse, if you're not gaining new skills and you are doing work that is not challenging you, own your career and ask for some growth opportunities. If that is not possible and it is increasingly clear that you will be doing the same work with no hope for growth, it is time to move on. Don't let your professional six-pack of skills turn into a flabby spare tire. This attitude can creep into other areas of your life as well. None of us has reached the pinnacle of our existence doing work we don't care about.

8. You Have No Interest in Moving Up the Ladder

If you would rather jump into a sleeping bag with twenty flea-infested squirrels than consider taking on your boss's job, that's a problem. If the thought of doing his job is causing you anxiety because you hate the work and you have no interest working with the jokers at the next level, that's another reason to consider moving on.

9. You Spend Your Time Outside of Work Rehashing the Negative Aspects of Your Job

Are Sunday nights the worst night of the week, thinking about the workweek ahead? Do you spend your family vacations rehashing the misery of your work team? Do your parents, your significant other, and your kids know the names of everyone you despise on your work team? If so, you are likely spending far too much time outside of work dwelling on the negative aspects of your job.

BUT, I'M NOT A QUITTER!

Let's say that you wanted to take a road trip from New York City to Los Angeles. If you started your trip driving full speed toward Miami, it is safe to say that you are driving in the wrong direction.

Once you realize where you're headed, wouldn't it make sense to stop, change direction, and drive west toward Los Angeles? No reasonable person would call you a "quitter" because you stopped driving toward Miami. If anything, you should be applauded for having the sense to change direction once you realized that you were going the wrong way.

Unfortunately, the opposite seems to happen in the real world, doesn't it? In the real world, you're expected to finish what you start *no matter what.* Even if that means driving full speed toward Miami when you're really trying to get to Los Angeles.

That makes no sense.

It makes just as little sense to keep plowing ahead in a job that is detracting from your health, your personal relationships, and your sanity just because you don't want to be labeled a quitter. Why would you keep going if you were driving in the wrong direction?

We are here to make the workplace work and, unfortunately, there will be times when we will need to do that elsewhere. If you have made that determination, it has nothing to do with being a quitter or being mentally soft. It is solely about one thing—making better choices.

A Chinese proverb says, "Of all strategies, knowing when to quit may be the best."

I agree.

CHAPTER

17

POSITIVITY FOREVER:

The End of the Beginning

One day your heart will stop beating, and none of your fears will matter. What will matter is how you lived.

—HENRI JUNTTILA

Every movement that has changed the world started with three clear visions.

The first is a real, unfiltered vision of our current state of affairs. The second is a beautiful vision of what our future could look like if we did the work to improve our current state of affairs. This entire book has been focused on these two visions.

What I haven't explored yet is the third vision that serves as my primary motivation to make this movement a reality. The third and final vision is the terrifying reality of what our future will look like if we do nothing.

Yes, I am motivated by pain.

It's what keeps me up at night, it wakes me up every morning and it keeps me going when I want to quit. It is what kept me writing this book, it is why I keep showing up to do the necessary work, and it is what inspires me to lead this movement when it would be much easier not to do it.

I'm not just referring to my pain. I'm also referring to the pain of others.

I have seen the tears. I have seen once-healthy bodies ravaged by illness. I have seen families irreparably broken. I have seen amazingly talented individuals walk away from work that could benefit the world. I have seen the good guys lose and the bad guys win.

I have seen enough.

The path that our society is currently on is not sustainable. We will destroy ourselves if we continue to overwork ourselves to exhaustion, choose profits over kindness and mutual respect, and accept bullying and incivility as the price for working in a grown-up world.

This insanity has to stop, and that's why we are here. Getting large groups of people to change through big and flashy company initiatives is great, but real sustainable change happens at the individual level, one person at a time. That change starts with us. This is the tipping point at which we get to decide where we are headed as a society, and we get to lead the way.

Or not.

Either way, this movement has officially begun. The decision that you make next will carry enormous implications for this movement, for the future of the world, and for your life.

And it's on your shoulders, my friend.

CRAFTING YOUR LEGACY

To help you to decide what to do next, I want to you think about what happens at the end of your life.

Have you ever spent time with someone who is on his deathbed? Have you ever looked deeply into the eyes of someone who is days, hours, or minutes away from leaving this earth?

If so, you know the one thing these people have in common: They fully understand that the only thing that matters—and has ever mattered—are the people in their lives.

On your deathbed, your college degrees, your job titles, and the fact that you landed the corner office in your workplace are all utterly meaningless. You won't ask to have your Mercedes-Benz rolled into the hospital room so you can gaze at it and smell the leather interior one last time. No one is going to read your resume at your funeral.

In your final moments, the only thing that will matter is how you lived. That's it. That is what people will remember about you long after you are gone, and you are writing that story for them right now. Did you make other people's lives better because of your conscious presence in their lives, or did you do the opposite? That's your legacy.

Don't make the woeful choice to wait until you are on your deathbed to start taking your legacy seriously. We are here to do much more than repeatedly step on people's necks and throw unsuspecting colleagues under the bus until we die. We are not here to kiss as much ass as we can and sell our soul to the person with the highest job title until we die. We are certainly not here to treat other people's lives as if they were insignificant means to our self-involved ends until we die.

We are here to fully connect with other people by treating others with kindness and love. Yeah, I said it, *love.* That is what matters when people have the clarity of death staring them in the face, and I believe we should use that example for how to live personally and professionally while we still have plenty of life left.

What if I'm wrong about everything? That is a risk I am willing to take. I would rather know that I added to the total of love and kindness in my workplace and in the world, than chose to do nothing. Isn't this the only option that makes sense? It is the clearest path to a more meaningful work experience and a more positive world for all of us.

We will leave a legacy behind when we leave the earth—that fact is unavoidable. I'm not waiting until then. I'm here to leave a positive legacy after I leave every room I enter while I'm alive.

As Solutionists, this is our primary goal.

THE ONLY THING THAT CAN STOP US

There is only one thing that can stop us from making our work work.

Is it the ABCs, incivility, or overwork? No. This problem is more sinister than all of those other things combined.

It's apathy.

Yes, apathy—the lack of interest, enthusiasm, or concern about the seriousness of this issue—is the biggest challenge to improving the world. I'm not sure where this lack of interest, enthusiasm, or concern comes from. Maybe we believe that improving the working world is someone else's job. It's not. If it is up to someone else, who is this person and why hasn't she done anything about it yet? We need to stop kidding ourselves—the work is yours and it's mine.

We have the blueprint. World-changing movements have already been led by people like Martin Luther King, Jr., Nelson Mandela, Mother Teresa, and Mahatma Gandhi. It is time to stop deifying these leaders. Each of them did not achieve incredible results by being anointed as one of the "special ones" destined to positively change our world. They are no more special than you or I, and if they were alive they would tell you that.

Their edge is that they gave a damn. They cared enough to keep moving forward, despite the obstacles, setbacks, drama, and well-positioned opposition that tried to crush them along the way. And they won, too—not because of their talent, but because they cared.

So do you give a damn about this? Do you care enough about altering the course of the working world by leading by example and helping others do the same? If not, I can promise you that apathy will win.

But if we care enough about this movement, each other, and the future of the world, then we will win.

THE SPOON AND THE OCEAN

Defeating apathy is not going to be easy. The path to creating a more positive working world is littered with the corpses of many well-meaning men and women who failed to reach the mountaintop. Apathy killed off most of them.

The enormity of this task is enough to make a coward out of any hero. Who are we to create an environment of kindness and mutual respect at our jobs and, even crazier, use that as the spark to create a movement of workplace positivity throughout the world? It is much easier to declare this impossible and not to care about the outcome, because doing so will make it hurt so much less when we fail to achieve it.

But what if we don't fail and this wasn't impossible? What if the spark to change the world lived within each of us? We don't need superhuman strength, a prestigious job title, or fearlessness. We just need a reminder of what the human spirit is capable of achieving.

Let this story be your reminder.

One day a man dreamed of doing the impossible.

He desperately wanted to change the world in a positive way, and after years of just talking about it, he was now finally ready to do something about it.

As soon as he was ready to take action on his dream, the villain in the story appeared.

The villain's name was Apathy.

Apathy decided to play a game with the man. Apathy's motive was a simple one: to destroy the man's spirit before he took any action to achieve his dream.

The villain looked sternly at the man and said, "If you're serious about doing the impossible, prove it to me."

The man nodded as Apathy led him to the beach. The villain smirked as he handed the man a spoon and a bucket.

"Empty it. The whole ocean. Use this spoon and bucket to get started."

The man paused as he looked out at the ocean.

Enormous.

Expansive.

Deep.

Impossibly huge.

The villain smiled because it was obvious that the man was ready to give up before he even started. The man's spirit was clearly broken.

The villain was wrong.

The man defiantly got down on his hands and knees and started to spoon the ocean into his bucket one spoonful at a time.

The villain began to laugh at the man.

The man kept spooning.

All of a sudden, the villain looked concerned as a curious onlooker walked toward the man.

She had a spoon and a bucket.

She knelt down beside the man and started to spoon the

ocean into her bucket, too. She brought a friend with her who did the same.

The villain's concern suddenly turned into fear. The man and his new friends had to be stopped for the villain to survive, and the villain knew it.

The villain tried to discourage the man and his friends by telling them that the task was impossible. The ocean cannot be emptied. If it were possible, it would have been done by someone else by now.

At that moment, the villain caught a break. Storm clouds moved in and heavy rain started to fall.

The villain then smiled confidently as the downpour continued to fall on their heads. All their hard work had been for nothing.

The villain laughed more loudly than before.

The villain's laughter stopped instantly when it was clear that the group was not listening to the laughter.

They chose to use the rainstorm as an opportunity to bond more closely together. As the rain fell harder, their dedication grew stronger.

And they kept spooning, even in the pouring rain.

Their enthusiasm for this incredible task was contagious, as more people from all walks of life joined in with their spoons and buckets.

There was now a visible difference in the ocean.

Excitement began to build and the rest of the world wanted to be part of the process. Millions of people came to the ocean with their spoons and their buckets to participate in something bigger than themselves.

The villain could no longer reach these people.

The group had now become a movement.

Apathy's voice had been rendered irrelevant by the millions of excited "spooners," each doing their little part to change the world.

The ocean was now empty.

The villain was defeated.

The world was officially changed forever.

And it all started with a belief that it could be done and by a single person picking up a spoon to do the impossible, one spoonful at a time.

Is it really that simple for each of us to change the world in our own special way?

I think so.

Conclusion

How wonderful it is that no one need wait a single moment before starting to improve the world.

—ANNE FRANK

I can still remember the surreal sensation of my humanity flowing back into my body after the near-attempt to take my own life. As I sat in my car on the side of the freeway, it was as if I had been figuratively hanging upside down for hours with no blood circulation to my legs, and then the world gently placed me right-side up again.

It was joyous to be able to feel something again.

It only took a few minutes, but as the life flowed back to my soul, the utter meaninglessness that had once enveloped my entire body like a thick haze, disappeared completely. The meaninglessness was replaced by a new world I did not recognize. A world where I could make a difference. A world that required something of me.

It did not call for me to acquire positional power or to get another college degree. This new world, blurred by my tears, only called for me to do one simple thing.

Be real.

I needed to get brutally real about what I was going to do with this gift that had been given to me: the gift of a second chance. How many people get a second chance? I don't know, but I sure as hell was not going to waste a minute of the one I had been given.

So much changed in my life after that incident, but the one word that kept replaying in my mind was *regret.* I knew that I would regret not doing something—anything—to help create a working world where we treated each other better. Waiting to be ready to do this was no longer an option. I feared doing nothing more than I feared my lack of skills, strategic connections, thoughtful planning, or readiness.

The plan was to jump and sprout wings on the way down. Or crash and burn. Truthfully, I was okay with either option—I was just no longer okay with standing still. Avoiding regret is a powerful motivator, and it gave me the nudge off the cliff that I needed to see if I could fly.

I believe that we all have wings but, for many of us, they are hidden under an armored shell of accumulated pain, bitterness, and hopelessness. I wore it, so I know. I also know that I was not alone—millions of people all over the world build their own special armored suit as protection from the rudeness, incivility, and bullying they are enduring on a daily basis.

Think of that—*millions of people* who are grounded with no idea that they can fly. Mainly because they are too busy shielding themselves from attacks from their own colleagues to realize that beautiful wings are hidden under their self-created armor. This is a crime against humanity.

I'm on the side of humanity, so that's why I'm fighting against this crime. In the past few years, I have encountered many others who have chosen to join with me in creating a kinder and more respectful world at work, and I am exceedingly thankful for their encouragement, resilience, and unbreakable strength. Together, we have been able to fly higher than we ever thought possible.

Isn't that what this is all about?

There is no more meaningful act than to help others realize that they can fly and, once they come to that realization, to help them to fly as high as possible. I didn't see that world before, but I see it now. I now know what it means to be truly alive and to deeply connect with a meaningful cause, with other like-minded revolutionaries, and with a world that needs positivity more than ever.

Regardless of your situation, you can take the first step to make this new world a reality.

This is how we will make the workplace work.

Notes

Chapter 1

1. "Little Change in U.S. Employee Engagement in January" (February 8, 2016), www.gallup.com/poll/189071/little-change-employee-engagement-january.aspx?g_source=EMPLOYEE_ENGAGEMENT&g_medium=topic&g_campaign=tiles.
2. "How to Tackle U.S. Employees' Stagnating Engagement," (June 11, 2013), www.gallup.com/businessjournal/162953/tackle-employees-stagnating-engagement.aspx.
3. Gary Namie, Ph.D "2014 WBI U.S. Workplace Bullying Survey," (2014), www.workplacebullying.org/multi/pdf/WBI-2014-US-Survey.pdf: 5.

Chapter 2

1. Christine Pearson and Christine Porath, "The Price of Incivility," *Harvard Business Review* (January–February 2013), https://hbr.org/2013/01/the-price-of-incivility.
2. Christine Pearson and Christine Porath, *The Cost of Bad Behavior: How Incivility is Damaging Your Business and What to Do About It* (New York: Penguin, 2009), iBooks Edition.
3. Alan H. Rosenstein MD MBA, Michelle O'Daniel MHA MSG, "A Survey of the Impact of Disruptive Behaviors and Communication Defects on Patient Safety," *The Joint Commission Journal on Quality and Patient Safety*, Volume 34 Number 8 (August 2008): 465–466
4. Pearson and Porath, "The Price of Incivility," https://hbr.org/2013/01/the-price-of-incivility.

Chapter 4

1. Deborah Norville, *The Power of Respect: Benefit from the Most Forgotten Element of Success* (Thomas Nelson, 2009), iBooks Edition.

Chapter 6

1. Rebecca Ray, Milla Sanes, and John Schmitt, "No-Vacation Nation Revisited," Center for Economic and Policy Research, (May 2013): 2.
2. Marc Landy and Sidney M. Milkis, *American Government: Enduring Principles, Critical Choices* (Cambridge: Cambridge University Press, 2014): 155.
3. Glassdoor, "Q1 2014 Employment Confidence Survey," https://press-content.glassdoor.com/app/uploads/files_mf/ecsq114supplement.pdf: 1.

4. Ibid., 2.
5. Ellen Galinsky, James T. Bond, Stacy S. Kim, et. al, "Overwork in America: When the Way We Work Becomes Too Much," (New York: Families and Work Institute, 2005): 2.
6. Bureau of Labor Statistics, "American Time Use Survey" (October 26, 2015), *www.bls.gov/tus/charts/.*

Chapter 7

1. "Don't Believe Everything You Think," *Cleveland Clinic Wellness, http://www.clevelandclinicwellness.com/DailyDose/archive/2014/08/12/Dont-Believe-Everything-You-Think.aspx.*

Chapter 8

1. "Why Having Friends at Work Is Important," OfficeVibe (September 16, 2014), https://www.officevibe.com/blog/infographic-friends-at-work.

Chapter 9

1. Tom Rath and Donald Clifton, *How Full Is Your Bucket?: Positive Strategies for Work and Life* (New York: Gallup Press, 2004), Kindle Edition.
2. Ibid.
3. Globoforce Workforce Mood Tracker, "The Impact of Recognition on Employee Retention" (September 2011): 5.
4. Elizabeth Newton, "Overconfidence in the Communication of Intent: Heard and Unheard Melodies," PhD diss., Stanford University, 1990.
5. Janice Kaplan, "Gratitude Survey," John Templeton Foundation (June-October 2012): 2.

Chapter 11

1. "Workplace Bullying and Disruptive Behavior: What Everyone Needs to Know," Safety & Health Assessment and Research for Prevention Program (April 2011), www.lni.wa.gov/safety/research/files/bullying.pdf.
2. Workplace Bullying Institute, "Estimating the Costs of Bullying," http://www.workplacebullying.org/individuals/solutions/costs/.
3. Gary Namie, PhD "U.S. Workplace Bullying Survey" (September 2007): 10, http://workplacebullying.org/multi/pdf/WBIsurvey2007.pdf.

Chapter 15

1. Brené Brown, *Daring Greatly: How the Courage to be Vulnerable Transforms the Way We Live, Love, Parent and Lead* (New York: Penguin Random House, 2012), iBooks edition.

Acknowledgments

Maya Angelou once said, "There is no greater agony than bearing an untold story inside you." This is *so* true. The pain of writing this book was only exceeded by the agony of keeping it inside me for most of my adult life. I am not ashamed to admit that as I sat down to write this book, I was not strong enough to deal with that pain alone. Thankfully, I had a great deal of help to push me past the limits of what I believed was possible to get this book into your hands.

To my wife Amber—what can I say? There is no book and there is no movement without your love and support. You are the epitome of leadership and strength, and your example sustained me through each sleepless night that I spent plugging away at my laptop. My hope is that I made you as proud of me as I am of you every single day. I love you, babe.

To my daughters Kaya and Nia—I know that you both are too young to read this now, but I hope that by the time that you become career women, this book would have helped to create a kinder and more positive professional environment for you both. Daddy loves you more than googolplex Jupiters, and I will do anything in my power to fight for a future working world for you that is far more positive than what millions of people are experiencing now.

To my brothers Doyin and Femi—each day I looked at what you both have accomplished, and as I looked on in awe, it inspired me to dream bigger. Doyin, you have positively changed the world as an author and an activist, and you are the single biggest reason I finally decided to write this book—I owe you big-time, Twin. Femi, you positively changed the world as a wildly influential corporate executive and leader, and your example of servant leadership is what first helped me realize that it is possible to be an exceptionally effective leader and still be an incredibly caring person. It is an honor to stand shoulder to shoulder with you both on this journey. You are the best brothers a guy could ever ask for, and I love you.

Mom and Dad—thank you so much for your unwavering support and belief in me. Even when you both had many opportunities to lose faith in me, for some reason you never did. I plan on spending the rest of my life repaying you both for it. As I said in the dedication, this book is for you . . . and it's only the beginning. I love you both so much.

To Argelia Monroy, Clayton Vetter, Courtney Scarlata, Nicholas Ruhe, Reg Randles, and Sherry Dodge—thank you for being the best professionals I have ever had the honor of working with. No one besides the seven of us will know the countless battles we have fought (and won), the tears we have shed, and the infinite amount of joy and friendship we have shared together. You will have a place in the "core" of my life until the day I die. Thank you for allowing me to serve as your leader, but far more importantly, as your friend and biggest fan.

To Frances Black—you are truly the greatest literary agent there is on this planet. Your intelligence, insight, patience, and persistence are extraordinary, and I am so thankful for you and your sage wisdom throughout this entire process. I am not only a better writer, but also I am a better person for having you in my life.

To Blanca Oliviery, Kate Zimmermann, Marilyn Kretzer, Sari Murray, Trudi Bartow, and the rest of the fabulous Sterling Publishing team—there has not been a day since I signed my literary deal that I didn't feel like the luckiest guy in the world. Thank you for taking a chance on me by choosing to publish this book, for your constant professionalism, and for your kindness during this journey. Your team is a beautiful example of making work work.

To Kelly Gurnett—five years ago, I found your blog via a Google search and I was hypnotized by your unapologetically real writing style. It was after reading your blog for hours on end that I knew I had to become a writer, too. Thank you for being the inspiration that started my writing journey.

To the Solutionists at The Positivity Solution—thank you for your constant encouragement, and for helping me to believe that I could positively influence the world with my writing. Just three short years ago, I would never have imagined that this would be possible. To three Solutionists in particular, Donna Murray, Kathy McQuillan, and Sharon Ledwith—you always gave me enormous support and love throughout the journey with your consistently kind and thoughtful comments. I want you to know how much that means to me. Thank you so much.

Lastly, for the friends who have had my back since day one, the transcendent leaders who have showed me how to lead with love instead of fear (and the less-than-positive ones who did the opposite), and the mentors I have admired from afar (Brené Brown, Elizabeth Gilbert, E.T. the Hip-Hop Preacher, Gary Vaynerchuk, Les Brown, Marie Forleo, Michael Port, Oprah Winfrey, Pamela Slim, Prince Ea, Steven Pressfield, Tony Robbins, and Wayne Dyer, to name a few)—thank you for your help.

It is because of all of you that I was able to make this work.

About the Author

Shola Richards is a dynamic keynote speaker, an in-demand leadership trainer/consultant, an award-winning Director of Training, and a positivity blogger with a passionate worldwide following. He has personally trained thousands of employees on topics ranging from transformational leadership to creating high-functioning teams, and he has maintained a near-impossible 99.6 percent participant-satisfaction rating. His blog The Positivity Solution was created in May 2013, and his articles have been read by readers in over 160 countries and counting. His unshakable optimism and unquenchable passion for creating a more positive world at work and at home for millions of people have caught the attention of mainstream media. His work has been featured in *Black Enterprise*, *Business Insider Australia*, *Complete Wellbeing India*, *The Huffington Post*, and in numerous other publications all over the world, recognizing him as an expert on workplace happiness and engagement.

Additionally, Shola is a father, husband, identical twin, and a self-professed "kindness extremist" who will not rest until bullying and incivility is extinct from the American workplace.

You can follow Shola at www.thepositivitysolution.com
Facebook: https://www.facebook.com/ThePositivitySolution
Twitter: https://twitter.com/positivitysolve
Instagram: https://www.instagram.com/positivitysolve

Discussion Guide

1. Throughout *Making Work Work*, Shola Richards mentions the urgent need to create a positivity movement to change how we treat each other at work. He also redefines positivity at work as "the act of using kindness and mutual respect to create improved outcomes." Do you believe that it is possible to create a global positivity movement based on kindness and mutual respect in the workplace? Is this something the world urgently needs? Discuss this with your group.

2. Richards says in chapter 1, that "most people don't become miserable or disengaged in their jobs because they dislike the work they're doing—it's because they dislike the people they're doing the work with." Take a moment to reflect on your current workplace situation. Do you agree or disagree with his statement? What is the primary source of unhappiness and disengagement in your workplace?

3. In chapter 2, Richards introduces readers to an alien named Krej. What is the common workplace problem that Krej represents? Discuss this specific problem with your group. Have you experienced this problem in your workplace? If so, does this problem affect your work in the ways that are outlined by the research noted in chapter 2? Why do you think that many companies dismiss this problem, despite its proven and widespread negative effects?

4. In chapter 3, Richards introduces us to the term "Solutionist." Specifically, he says, "in a world full of problem pointers (aka, people who point out problems and do nothing else), Solutionists are the ones who are focused on being problem solvers and living each day as part of the solution in their professional and personal lives." Based on this definition, are you a Solutionist in your workplace? If so, why?

5. Throughout the book, Richards mentions the R.E.A.L. strategy as the way to create a culture of positivity in the workplace. What does the R.E.A.L. acronym stand for? Using your workplace as an example, do you believe that consistently addressing the four areas of the R.E.A.L. strategy could result in a significant positive change in your workplace? Why or why not?

6. What does Richards describe as the "lie that you've been told (and believed)"? Do you agree or disagree with his assertion?

7. Richards mentions in chapter 6 his disdain for the terms "work-life balance" and the more modern version, "work-life integration." What is the work-life term that he suggests instead, and do you believe that implementing it consistently would reduce your overall stress level at work and at home? What are your challenges in managing your work with the responsibilities of your personal life?

8. Setting clear priorities, enforcing boundaries, and saying NO are three necessary aspects of honoring yourself at work, according to Richards. Are these skills ones that you naturally perform well, or are these areas of struggle/challenge for you?

9. Have you ever said "yes" to a clear boundary violation at work, when you really wanted to say "NO"? If so, take a moment to share your situation with the group and what motivated you to say "yes" instead of "NO." If you were aware of the L.I.N.E. Strategy (introduced in chapter 6) before the boundary violation, would you have used that strategy on the boundary violator? Why or why not?

10. Richards introduces readers to the Attitude Adjustment Pyramid in chapter 7. Which level of the pyramid do you believe will be the most helpful for you to maintain a positive attitude during the challenging times at work? Why?

11. Do you believe that the workplace is an appropriate place to make friends? Discuss the role of friendship at work. Does it make for a more engaged workplace, or does it end up creating more problems in the workplace than it solves?

12. Richards mentions that we live and work in an "appreciation-starved society," and in chapter 9 he lists four reasons why many people fail to deliver meaningful appreciation at work. Which one of those four reasons do you see most commonly in your workplace?

13. Share an instance of when you have received sincere, specific, and meaningful appreciation from someone at work. What kind of impact did the appreciation have on you?

14. When Richards mentions in chapter 10, "if you cannot change something, the only positive option is acceptance," do you agree with him? What are your thoughts on accepting the things that you cannot change in the workplace?

15. Workplace bullying is defined as "repeated, unreasonable actions of individuals (or a group) directed toward an employee (or a group of employees), which are intended to intimidate, degrade, humiliate, or undermine; or which create a risk to the health or safety of the employee(s)." Based on this definition, have you ever been a victim of workplace bullying? Share your situation with the group, the specific behaviors that made it workplace bullying, the effects of the bullying on you/your health, and what (if anything) you did to resolve it.

16. The R.E.A.L. work assignment in chapter 12 challenges readers to have a "Complaint-Free Monday." If you tried it, was it easier than you thought it would be, harder than you thought it would be, or pretty much what you expected? Why? Share your biggest takeaway from completing this R.E.A.L. work assignment.

17. In chapter 13, Richards mentions that the biggest hurdle readers will need to overcome in order to make this movement a reality is the idea that they can choose to be leaders in this movement right now—with or without authority. Have you ever made significant positive change in your workplace without formal authority? Share a situation with the group.

18. In chapter 14, Richards lists five ways to ensure that the people you work with feel sincerely valued and important. Which one of the five strategies resonates the most with you, and why?

19. In chapter 15, when Richards figuratively mentions to the readers "I want you to kill yourself," what is the main message that he is trying to convey?

20. Have you put into practice all of the R.E.A.L. work assignments? What have you learned from putting these techniques into action in your workplace or professional life? Which assignment have you found to be the most challenging for you? Which assignment has had the most positive impact on you? Why?

Index